D1126368

ON INOCULATING MORAL PHILOSOPHY AGAINST GOD

The Aquinas Lecture, 2000

ON INOCULATING MORAL PHILOSOPHY AGAINST GOD

Under the auspices of the
Wisconsin-Alpha Chapter of Phi Sigma Tau

by

JOHN M. RIST

MARQUETTE
UNIVERSITY

PRESS

Library of Congress Cataloging-in-Publication Data

Rist, John M.
  On inoculating moral philosophy against God / by John
M. Rist.
      p. cm. — (The Aquinas lecture ; 2000)
Includes bibliographical references.
  ISBN 0-87462-167-4 (alk. paper)
  1. Religion and ethics. I. Title. II. Series.
  BJ47 .R57 2000
  170—dc21
                                                99-050978

© 1999 Marquette University Press
Printed in the United States of America

MARQUETTE UNIVERSITY PRESS
MILWAUKEE

The Association of Jesuit University Presses

Prefatory

The Wisconsin-Alpha Chapter of Phi Sigma Tau, the International Honor Society for Philosophy at Marquette University, each year invites a scholar to deliver a lecture in honor of St. Thomas Aquinas.

The 2000 Aquinas Lecture, *On Inoculating Moral Philosophy against God*, was delivered on Sunday, February 27, 2000, by John M. Rist, Professor Emeritus from the University of Toronto and currently residing in Cambridge, England.

John M. Rist was educated at Trinity College, Cambridge. He completed the Classical Tripos, Part 1 and Part 2, the latter with a specialization in ancient philosophy, in 1958 and 1959; he proceeded to the M.A. in 1963. He taught Greek at University College in the University of Toronto from 1959 to 1969. From 1969 to 1980 he was Professor of Classics at the University of Toronto. From 1980 to 1983 he was Regius Professor of Classics at the University of Aberdeen, and from 1983 to 1996 he returned to the University of Toronto as Professor of Classics and Philosophy, with a cross-appointment to St. Michael's College from 1983 to 1990. He become Professor Emeritus of the University of Toronto in 1997 and has been part-time Visiting Professor at the Institutum Patristicum Augustinianum in Rome since 1998.

In 1976 he was elected a Fellow of the Royal Society of Canada, and in 1991 he was elected a life member of Clare Hall, Cambridge. In 1995 he was

the Lady Davis Visiting Professor in Philosophy at
the Hebrew University in Jerusalem.

Professor Rist's publications include the follow-
ing books: *Man, Soul and Body: Essays in Ancient
Thought from Plato to Dionysius* (1996), *Augustine:
Ancient Thought Baptized* (1994), *The Mind of
Aristotle* (1989), *Platonism and Its Christian Heri-
tage* (1985), *Human Value: A Study of Ancient Philosophical Ethics* (1982), *On the Independence of Mat-
thew and Mark* (1978), *The Stoics* (1978), *Epicurus:
An Introduction (1972), Stoic Philosophy* (1969),
Plotinus: The Road to Reality (1967), and *Eros and
Psyche: Studies in Plato, Plotinus and Origen* (1964).
He has also published some eighty articles on an-
cient Greek philosophy, Hellenistic philosophy, Plo-
tinus and Neoplatonism, Patristics, and medieval
philosophy. To mention only a few of Professor Rist's
many articles, among the most important there are:
"The Nature and Background of Basil's
'Neoplatonism,'" in *Basil of Caesarea: Christian,
Humanist, Ascetic,* ed. P. J. Fedwick (1981); "Where
Else?" in *Philosophers Who Believe*, ed. Kelly J. Clark
(1993); "Plotinus and Christian Philosophy," in *The
Cambridge Companion to Plotinus,* ed. L. P. Gerson
(1996); and "Platonic Soul, Aristotelian Form,
Christian Person," in *Self, Soul and Body in Reli-
gious Experience,* ed. A. Baumgarten, J. Assmann,
and G. G. Stroumsa (1998).

To Professor Rist's distinguished list of publications, Phi Sigma Tau is pleased to add: *On Inoculating Moral Philosophy against God.*

On Inoculating
Moral Philosophy
against God

A. Philosophy and Theology

Perhaps they made a great mistake in the twelfth century; they attempted a clear separation of philosophy and theology.[1] But why should that be a mistake? Surely the difference is obvious (though it was not obvious to Augustine): philosophy starts with reason and is determined by argument; theology starts with revelation and attempts to clarify it. So, are we to suppose that natural theology would be philosophy and the philosophy of religion would be theology, even if by its failure to establish the clarity of any theological proposition it concludes to the non-existence of God? The question at least shows that the notion that philosophy—as we now understand it—can be separated methodologically from theology is not as transparent as it looks. But the methodological distinction can perhaps be presented more effectively. It may lie less in the starting point than in the difference between induction (or perhaps deduction) on the one hand, and clarification on the other. Let us start by briefly considering some further complications and ambiguities

about that. We shall soon realize that the separation
of theology and philosophy eventually led (and will
always lead) to strange and surprising results in ethics.

Historically, the thesis that theology is concerned
with the *clarification* of specifically "religious" material seems to have been adopted, and in some quar-
ters it led to the near-death of the subject, its disso-
lution into loose talk about the meaningfulness of
relationships or being nice to people, while for philosophy a purely procedural account—philosophy
proceeds logically by deduction or induction—seems
to be either trivial or question-begging, in that we
either conclude that we can infer the subject of philosophy from its form, or that its form just is its
subject-matter, or that every time we think of something or construct an argument we are doing philosophy. But if at the present moment I either am
or am not doing philosophy, there must be some
kind of thinking which is not philosophizing—and
that is still true if at the present moment I am philosophizing *badly*.

Let us explain some of the difficulties and apparent oddities in a little more detail. First, theology
and clarification: it brings us back both in theory
and in historical fact to the question, Clarification
of what? In the twelfth century the answer to that
probably seemed misleadingly simple. Theology
would involve the exegesis of the Bible and of
Church traditions, not least those embodied in the
decisions of the various Councils starting from
Nicaea. Such explications could be supported by
reference to more or less unchallenged theological

authorities, especially Augustine. But for reasons well enough known and which need not be rehearsed here, there soon came a time when the authority of those authorities and of the Church itself began to be challenged, and the claims of *sola Scriptura*, of the Scriptures alone, became dominant. But later still, in what would have been devastating to the founders of the Protestant revolution, the authority of the Bible itself was put in question: Form criticism and varieties of historical criticism in the nineteenth century, first in the German heartland of Protestantism, then more widely, began to destroy that very monument of authority which the Reformers had set up. With the Church long abandoned as adequate authority and the Bible itself now dissected, above all in the strange quest for the disappearing "historical Jesus," theology, which in the Reformation had tended to move from any connection with metaphysics towards Biblical exegesis alone, now found itself without stable subject matter, almost without substantive content. From faith alone in Christ, we moved to faith alone. But in what? In extreme cases only faith in man and his ideals. The prophet Feuerbach had arrived.

In the process Jesus was often reduced to a wise man, a teacher of morality—and then people also began to ask whether there is anything distinctive in Christian morality (not the same question as whether there is anything distinctive in the Christian version of strictly *theistic* morality), or is it merely a composite of wise sayings from the Jewish (or other) past? And two further questions arose: What is the basis of that morality, that is, could it be shown as at least intelligible good sense? and, Does it depend on the existence of God? Later still some began to talk of a "common morality," meaning something the core of which is supposed to be held in a post-Christian world by Jews, Christians, and decent ex-Christians alike.[2] But the problem of that common morality is perhaps less whether it is true than whether it can equip itself with any adequate intellectual defence of a sort common to Jews, Christians, and ex-Christians.

In talking about morality we are getting ahead of ourselves. I was observing that as a matter of history, soon after theology had to find a specific subject matter apart from philosophy, while still remaining a clarificatory art, it ran into peculiar difficulties. In the contemporary world, even where theologians avoid the death-trap of a mere Biblicism, other alternatives often seem hardly tasty. Extreme measures are often available: theology can turn into a mixture of canon law and casuistry, trying to apply the teaching of some only partially biblical authority, such as the Magisterium (in the modern sense of the word), to specific and normally pastoral problems in the contemporary world, and to the extent that this activity is carried on without reference to any rational investigation of its foundations, it will tend to degenerate into some variety of fideism and thus interest only those who want to fundamentalize; or— the opposite extreme—it will break itself down into a set of "theologies" (whether of art, politics, or even, absurdly, of God), each of which seems largely concerned to put some sort of benevolently "spiritual" spin on the activity on which it purports to theologize.

B. Form and Content in Philosophical Enquiry

It is not my present purpose to discuss theology, except in so far as, once divorced from philosophy, it often seems to become a wanderer, some kind of lost sheep. (The present pope's encyclical on Faith and Reason seems to wish to bring this to the attention of those who may feel obliged to attend to it.) Needless to say, such wanderings are inclined to earn the contempt not only of traditional believers but of much of the secular community—except when they serve the turn of that community by giving one of its fashionably pet projects a seal of spiritual approval. But after all, what else could be expected? The sheer fideism of a merely legalistic approach to theology has nothing to say to secular philosophers qua philosophers—except that they are (perhaps diabolically) misguided; while the theological "pastoralists," lacking any specific subject-matter of their own with which to engage in their task of clarification, have little alternative than to provide an apparently respectable religious backing for secular projects good, bad and indifferent. Even in the case of the good ones—if we can find some rationale for identifying a project as better or worse rather than merely different—the nature of their goodness will remain only minimally justified in the minds of their agents. But if I am not immediately concerned with what happens to theology apart from philosophy, I am concerned whether or at least in what way philosophy (or at least ethics) can exist apart from what I shall venture to call theology.

We have already suggested that philosophy is apparently not just thinking and arguing, for there are certainly types of thinking which are not philosophizing. When I am thinking about what horse it would be sensible to back with large sums of money in the Kentucky Derby, I am not, in most people's book, doing philosophy. So, philosophy seems to be some kind of thinking, but not just any kind of thinking. Perhaps, then, it is not thinking about what will happen, like who will win the Kentucky Derby, or what disaster will happen in the year 2000, but it is thinking concerned with why things which happen happen; that would make it less predictive than explanatory. But it does not provide just any explanation; to provide historical explanations or scientific explanations is not to be philosophical. Perhaps it is to test whether such explanations, and others of similar sorts, make sense outside their own sphere of reference, within some wider framework, and additionally to test whether the historical, scientific, or whatever explanations are merely rules of thumb by which we can show that if you do certain things you get certain effects. These effects would be quite specific in the case of science—sulphuric acid will always, it seems, in our spatio-temporal circumstances, dissolve pieces of wood—and less settled in the case of history: a governmental decision to declare war on a neighbouring state will normally issue in the fighting of battles of some sort. In these latter cases philosophy will be concerned with saying something like, What does it mean to say that X causes Y? In the former it will ask questions like, Is it possible to understand both historical and scientific talk within some wider framework that deals with the nature of truth and falsehood?

In the sort of cases we have considered, the apparently philosophical questions which arise seem to arise from an attempt to understand more deeply some existing set of propositions which cannot in themselves be called philosophical. These base-propositions—a check on the history of philosophy will apparently confirm—do not arise from philosophical investigations, nor are they purely formal. It is true that at an advanced stage of philosophical enquiry it has been suggested by some that philosophical content—perhaps especially in ethics — can be derived from purely formal considerations, and we shall return to this in a moment, but first some of the early philosophical questions. For since we all agree that Parmenides, Socrates and Aristotle were philosophers, can we not also agree that what they do is philosophy?

Parmenides notoriously said that everything is and that we cannot properly say that not-being exists. Whatever we think of their quality, it is not hard to agree that these are philosophical statements. But they are certainly not "primitive" statements: both of them suggest that we already know what we are talking about when we speak of a thing, or that we have some idea of what is the difference between being and not being. And we have these ideas because we can point to specific things and say that they are there or that they are not there (or somewhere). Similarly with Socrates: let us suppose that

he said that we should look after our souls to ensure
that they are as good as possible. That presupposes
some idea of what we mean by a soul and of what
we might understand as goodness. In short, there
seems to be no philosophical question which is not
an attempt to understand some apparent piece of
already acquired knowledge or belief. And the problem with that is that the answers to all philosophical questions are to an important degree governed
by the nature of the questions asked. That is why
the history of philosophy can often be understood
not as a continuous progression, but as a series of
answers, first to one set of problems, then to another. And the more sets of problems there are, the
easier it becomes to generate a further set by rear-
ranging the already existing combinations—and that
is even without reference to completely new questions being asked. And of course there are completely
new questions: it was probably a completely new
question that was asked by Plato in enquiring, "Is
there such a thing as an immaterial substance?"

It might be suggested that the nature of philosophical enquiry changed dramatically as soon as
some kind of formal logic was discovered. Before
that philosophical questions could not be derived
from formal considerations; later they could be.
Once Aristotle had identified the law of contradiction and the law of excluded middle, it had become
possible to think in a quite different way. Of course
in one sense this is true: after Aristotle propositions
can be formally tested for identified types of unintelligibility, and those which fail the tests can be dismissed as of no philosophical interest. But Aristotle's

own attitude to his successes in logical formalizing was certainly not to suppose that he could now derive content from form. Indeed he did not think of logic as philosophy at all; it is merely a way of separating pseudo-questions from real questions, pseudo-arguments from real arguments. Nor, once he had decided that metaphysics need not be coterminous with Platonic speculation about Forms, did Aristotle suppose that any logical enquiry would simply eliminate the science of metaphysics altogether; it would rather help the philosopher to distinguish good metaphysics from bad. It had become a way of identifying and clarifying possible metaphysical propositions, possible metaphysical facts, as a necessary preamble to identifying whether those particular facts are true.

So, it begins to look as though the idea that philosophy can be distinguished from theology in its use of reason alone runs up against a very serious difficulty: philosophical reason is always to be exercised on propositions which contain assumptions, and indeed particular sets of assumptions. It has sometimes been supposed that the ethics of Kant provides a powerful exception to this rule, but that is not the case. According to Kant all moral propositions have to be such that we can will them to be a universal law, binding on all rational beings, no exceptions being made for ourselves. Or in more common jargon, moral principles must be universalizable.

It has sometimes been supposed that this procedure enables us to derive the content of moral propositions, for example, that they must all be in accord with the notion that persons must be treated always as ends in themselves and never merely as means. But whatever Kant's view of this—a matter on which there appear to be radically conflicting opinions—what he seems to have done is to argue the formal point that all moral propositions must be universalizable and then to have discovered (rather than shown) that all moral principles which are indeed universalizable in his sense in fact turn out to be such as to indicate that persons shall be valued as ends in themselves rather than as mere means. Thus if universalizability is a sufficient *condition* of moral judgments, then however many judgments pass the test, they will all be such as to value the person as an end in himself.

Whatever Kant thought—and I do not claim to know what he thought—the judgment that persons should be treated as ends is not merely another formulation of the law that moral judgments are universalizable, but the formulation of an apparent result of straining possible moral judgments for universalizability, which gives the result—which Kant happened to like—that persons should be treated as ends and not as mere means. In fact, the somewhat strange claim that only those judgments are properly moral in which *no kind* of exception is made for one's interest is itself guaranteed as a principle of morality by the circular claim that it leads to the result—which, as I said, Kant likes—that people should be treated as ends in themselves and not merely as means to ends. Since Kant's methodology enables him to claim that all special emphasis on one's own "happiness" is outside morality—and thereby to reject as non-moral a whole series of ethical claims which go back to Socrates—there seem likely to be special reasons why the conclusions about persons as ends and not means should be so curiously important for him.

It has been widely believed that these reasons result both from Kant's enthusiastic acceptance of the claims of Rousseau about the equality of man and from a basic axiom of the pietistic Christianity in which he was reared, namely, that man has been created in the image and likeness of God. If any of that is true, then so far from Kant deriving the content of an ethic from a purely formal principle, he has in fact found a formal principle which seems (to him) to generate and support a theory-loaded principle of which he approves for reasons which have nothing to do with logical form and everything to do with philosophical judgement about the nature and content of ethical thinking.

All this is by way of a rather easy-going and sketchy preamble, but it is designed to suggest, if not to demonstrate, that attempts to separate philosophy in general (and ethics in particular) from varieties of theological enquiry by way of their methodology (the one starts with reason, the other is concerned with the clarification of specific sorts of data—provided we can agree what that data is) are unlikely to be true. But surely, it will be said, the whole history of post-Cartesian philosophy would suggest that a distinction of this sort—at least that philosophy really does start simply from pure reason—is on the right lines. In fact, however, consideration of Descartes shows that precisely the opposite is the case. Descartes' use of purely formal principles—in his case the principle that every proposition should be doubted until one comes up with a proposition which cannot intelligibly be doubted—tells a story in relevant respects similar to Kant's. Prescind from the question whether Descartes' basic proposition "I exist" is in fact question-begging about the "I," or whether it is in any case basic enough because even if not basic what matters is that it cannot intelligibly be denied, and recognize that Descartes' method is precisely not to generate facts but to test apparent facts. Indeed he seems to think that an apparently false (if not unintelligible) "fact" is basic, namely, that I am immediately (and not—rightly or wrongly—by inference) aware of a pure core "self" or centre of consciousness, apart from that of which I am conscious.

C. An Augustinian Proposal

If not simply by methodology, then philosophy must (after all) be distinguished from theology—assuming that theology is not a pseudo-science like astrology—at least in part by subject-matter. But I do not want to labour the apparently familiar (if possibly vacuous) point of saying that philosophy starts with the world, while theology starts with God. Instead I intend to limit the scope of the discussion first by making an Augustinian claim about subject-matter and then by restricting my enquiries, as my title will have suggested, to the relationship between a limited area of philosophy and certain specific parts of theology. I would certainly suspect that if my approach works in this area it might be of some help in determining the more general relationship between philosophy and theology, but I have no intention of pursuing this wider enquiry here— nor of raising the even broader methodological question of whether if my approach will not do for some, even the major, branches of philosophy and theology, there is reason to suppose that it will at least be satisfactory for ethics.

The simple "Augustinian" attitude I should want to consider—though Augustine who does not distinguish between theology and philosophy would not have made it in the precise form in which I advance it—is that theology is an advanced form of philosophy, a philosophy, that is, in which more data is available (even though by "belief" and "in hope" rather than by knowledge). Historically speaking, indeed, though I call this attitude "Augustinian," and though Augustine made perhaps the most powerful use of it, he did not originate it. Rather it was the mind of the early Church at least from some time in the second century, in the days, let us say, of Justin Martyr, when Christians, increasingly aware that the end of the world was not yet and that they would unfortunately have to confront pagans for some time, began to realize that it would be helpful if, in a world composed much more largely of cultural "Hellenes," that is, those brought up in the Greek tradition of philosophy, than of Jews, they were to attempt some kind of explanation of their new religion which might make sense to the intellectual élites and opinion-formers of the predominant culture.

Thus the proponents of "Christian" or "true" philosophy, the product of an age at the same time beginning to develop a more systematic presentation of its own revealed truths—an age in which the prime such concern was with the relation of the Logos-Son-Messiah to the Father—came to recognize that pagan thinkers were not going to be persuaded to change their hostile estimate of Christianity merely by being preached at and told, without argument, to "believe."[3] Broadly speaking, however, the Christian thinkers had two options, both of which had at least the considerable advantage, they hoped, of forcing Christianity on their opponents' attention, of compelling them, as it were, to become used to it, even as an unpleasant option—but perhaps that unpleasantness would wear off a bit with time, habituation, and familiarity. Psychologically there is a sense in which there is an "argument" for Christianity in the mere fact of its visible and audible presence; contemporary non-Christians in various parts of the present world are also aware of this in their attempts—no honourable status for toleration here—to prevent their societies from being contaminated by Christianity.

The two options available for early Christians were either to argue (sophistically) from the multiplicity of the pagan philosophical schools that philosophy thus far was failing to come up with the right answers to the "big questions," or more plausibly from the antinomies generated within each school in turn that none of the approaches currently available had in fact been very successful; or they might combine this approach—and the more learned they became

the more they could begin to do this successfully—
with arguing that the difficulties which the pagan
thinkers were finding insuperable were caused less
by technical problems of logic and coherent thinking as such; rather they were caused by an insuffi-
ciency of data. In effect such Christians were claiming (almost in the spirit of Nagel's introduction to
The View from Nowhere) that the human mind could
not assemble, from its ordinary methods of argument and enquiry, whether empirical or dialectical,
the data necessary to come up with the results it
sough—of whatever nature such results might be.

To think in this way, as I have said, is peculiarly
patristic and very specifically Augustinian: Augustine tells us in the *Confessions* that the Platonists—
by his time some variety of Platonism was the pre-
ferred philosophical flavour for most Christian
thinkers—could go thus far and no further. They
could, by metaphysical reasoning, excogitate knowledge of God and his Word, but they could form no
notion of the Incarnation (or, as he would doubtless have been happy to add, of the Resurrection of
the flesh). But perhaps the best example of such an
attitude—an attitude, let me repeat, whereby Christian philosophy takes off from pagan philosophy and
completes it—is both proposed and analysed by the
third-century Greek thinker Origen. Origen's example—and Augustine's practice is frequently similar—is particularly relevant to the contemporary
study of ethics in that the strength of his case lies in
his claim that with the best will in the world, pagan
thought is riddled with difficulties of such a sort
that only new "Christian" data can resolve them. If

he is right, then if in any philosophical area, let us say in ethics, difficulties seem to be foundational, recurrent, and only resolvable with the addition of "Christian data," it will be useless and silly for the Christian thinkers to limit themselves to the data and methodologies available to the pagans—because then they will themselves be enmeshed in the same problems as the pagans.

Here is Origen's example (*Contra Celsum* 4.62-70). The Platonist Celsus had challenged the Christians over the problem of evil. Origen's reply is developed in three stages: first he shows that Celsus, though a purported Platonist, is professionally inadequate: he does not know the whole of Plato's position on the subject of evil: that subject—apparently unbeknown to Celsus—is treated in more than one place in Plato's writings. Second, Origen points out, Celsus is not a serious thinker but merely a sectarian or ideologist: or he would know that the best philosophical treatment of the topic of evil is in fact to be found not among the Platonists but in the book *On Good and Evil* by the Stoic Chrysippus. In the end, however, Chrysippus also fails—which brings Origen to part three of his response. Far from deriding the philosophers, the Christian should point out that they are failing because they are attempting the impossible. The problem of evil, according to Origen, cannot be solved without some knowledge—unavailable to unaided reason even in the distinguished Chrysippus, but in itself perfectly intelligible—of the fall of the angels.

The moral of the story—obviously—is this: that if there is any truth in Revelation, then there will be many areas of human thought—and ethics will al-most certainly be one such area—in which the law written on the human heart—the natural law, if you will—will of itself take us thus far and no further. Two consequences will follow: first that the common ground between Christian and non-Christian thinkers will be insufficient to allow agreement to be reached over either the first principles of ethics or the application of those first principles in certain areas. Second, that even if we should find that in certain practical areas of applied ethics there is apparent agreement between Christian and non-Christian thinkers, we should not be deluded by that agreement into supposing that it indicates either that the *justifications* for that common action will be similar for Christian and non-Christian alike, or that in fact there will not be important areas where agreement will not be possible at all—and precisely because in those areas the Christian is pursuing his principles to their logical limits while the secularist or neo-pagan is refusing to do so—or, indeed, because he is ultimately basing his behaviour on a very different, and incompatible, set of first principles.

I shall be maintaining that such is indeed part of the contemporary scene in ethics. If I am right, it would follow, *inter alia*, that one of the functions of the natural law, and of the surviving natural conscience (so to speak), in so far as it exists in men of good will, is to show us, like the Mosaic Law in the thought of Paul and Augustine, that we are of ourselves unable to understand the nature of morality, just as the Law is able to show us that we are sinners and not that we are able to avoid sin—indeed that under our own steam we are unable to avoid it.

At first sight the resulting picture would be discouraging and would display a number of threatening features. We should know that in debating questions of ethics with serious non-Christians (that is, apart from those who make Christian assumptions within an apparently anti-Christian mindset or, in some extended sense, metaphysic, a group to whom we shall return), we cannot expect agreement on many major topics, hence that our position in an increasingly post-Christian Western intellectual society will become all the more uncomfortable, and we shall be tempted to retreat (or maybe will be driven to retreat) into an intellectual ghetto. From this feeling of discomfort, this sense of being under threat, various ways of escape will present themselves: we may attempt to delude ourselves about the depth of our disagreements, and at the same time try to conceal them by not talking about those areas of ethics where we disagree, and on which—in accordance with our own first principles—we *should* disagree; or we may attempt to restrict the areas of disagreement by taking on board certain secular principles and attitudes which would diminish those disagreements, but at the cost of eventually undermining our entire ethical stance. Or alternatively, avoiding a Christian intellectual ghetto, we may merely become discouraged, realizing that the struggle to maintain our position, even if we have reason to believe that it is intellectually respectable, is unending. We feel trapped like Sisyphus, forever rolling his stone uphill only to see it roll back again.

Let me make an institutional parallel to indicate why that giving way to discouragement would apparently be wrong. In antiquity (as in various more modern societies), for Christians as well as for pagans, there was an institution called slavery. It seemed that society could not function well without the payment of such a price; indeed it is quite plausible that most of the artistic and philosophical achievement of the ancient world could not have been achieved without reliance on slave institutions—just as much modern art could not exist without the moral—and specifically sexual—corruption of adolescents in training. That, as Augustine would put it, is part of the darkness of social life: little good without toleration of other people's harms.

Moralists both Christian and pagan normally—indeed almost unanimously—reacted to the ancient phenomenon of slavery by urging masters to treat their slaves well: what mattered, they urged, was inner freedom, not external constraint, a doctrine easier for masters to hold than for slaves, though some slaves certainly held it. In part, as we know, such an attitude derives from the fact that in antiquity there is very little sense of what we would call, in secular jargon, systemic injustice, or in more papal language "structures of sin": no-one had yet read Max Weber. But also, especially in Christian writers deeply conscious of the endemic weakness of the human moral agent after the fall, above all therefore in Augustine, there was a certain sense that, even if the existing state of chattel slavery were to be abolished, other equally obnoxious forms of *dominatio* would soon arise to replace it; Augustine would have much sympathy with more recent notions of wage-slavery. And that sympathy, extended more widely, would not be misplaced. There does seem little reason to suppose that our desire to dominate one another will disappear or probably even diminish; certainly new forms of tyrannizing over others are likely to proliferate and show little sign of passing away. But such facts—if they are facts—of course in no way licence an individual to give up trying to improve present conditions, including institutional conditions. What they do, however, is make that task more difficult in so far as the struggle would seem to be unending: that, apparently, is a peculiarly difficult feature of the Christian vocation.

Thus then the institutional parallel. In reverting to the case of the individual thinker, we see that his case is analogous. He is condemned to be arguing in a secular universe and in doing so to be endlessly deploying the same arguments to new faces, like parents who have an infinite number of children, to each of whom in turn they have to rehearse familiar teaching in something of the following form. The following paralogism, they have to say, is not a syllogism: I want to sleep with my girlfriend: the Church does not approve of that; therefore God does not exist (or—less strikingly— the Church's teaching on fornication is deeply flawed). Right?

Let us assume that we have made at least a prima facie case for the claim that Christian thinking could be an extension of secular thinking, that it may be possible to argue that Christian thinking could therefore provide a better basis for the truth of secular thinking where secularists have—for whatever rea-

son—come up with the right answers, that therefore we cannot assume that we have identifiable first
principles in common with secularists and that we
cannot accept their first principles unless in the strict-
est sense we are aware of the condition of such acceptance. That condition is to suppose—at least for
the sake of argument—that God does not exist. But
how then can we more reasonably test whether there
is such a Christian extension of secular thinking as
we have proposed?

We could proceed more historically, showing that
as a matter of fact much Christian ethics has been
built upon certain pagan positions and has then extended them, just as Augustine thought that Christian metaphysics could be built on Platonism, and
that the extended structure could then be used to
test and rebuild some of the more shaky foundations of its Platonic base. But if we were to go along
that route, which I shall attempt very sketchily at a
later stage in the discussion, we should find that it
is not just any philosophical framework within
which Christian thinkers can work, but a version of
the system of Plato, adapted and reformed particularly in the areas of what we should now call theory
of action by the much more detailed labours of
Aristotle, while still, in respect of the importance of
a providential and transcendent God, in essence and
in core Platonic. And it will be one of the insistent
claims in passing of this present essay that it is vain
for Catholic philosophers to forget the residually
Platonic account both of man (that he is primarily
a being in moral space, to use the language of Charles
Taylor[4]), and of God (that he is an active, providen-

tial and transcendent agent). Obviously that latter doctrine was corrected, developed, enriched, and expanded by Christian writers, but its philosophical roots, we shall insist, should not be forgotten, lest, as it were, it wither on the postmodern vine.

D. Sacred and Profane Ethics

I do not intend to go down the historical route, investigating the historical development of Christian ethics, except for a few diversions along the way. Rather, I want to approach the question of the nature of useful debate between Christian and secular moral philosophers in a more systematic way, above all by raising three basic questions. The first concerns the way in which we can begin to debate first principles of ethics at all; the second is, "Are there any necessary Christian virtues of a sort which must be impossible, indeed must be mere delusions, to a secular thinker?" the third—not unrelated—is, "Are there any features of God, if he exists in a specially Christian form, which permeate not just the peculiarly Christian virtues, but the Christian concept of virtue as a whole?" In other words, was Augustine right in distinguishing virtue (that is, Christian virtue) from what we should dub "virtue" (in scare-quotes), and if so what precisely and specifically is at the root of the distinction? If we can answer these questions, we can also consider in what precisely systematic sense and on what precise philosophical terms Christian moral philosophy can and cannot be an extension of non-Christian thought. Or perhaps how much non-Christian ethics may be a foundationless shadow of something more theistic.

*

There have been, among Western philosophers, two common ways of approaching the question, What is a man? The answers are that a man is either a moral (and/or spiritual—I use moral in this extended sense) agent, or that a man is some sort of ontological whole, or as Aristotle—who typically talks in this mode—might like to put it, a composite of body and soul—prescinding therefore from the question whether "soul" or at least "human soul" is only fully intelligible within some reference to moral agency. But why do we think we are moral agents at all? With this question we approach the most difficult problems of ethics.

In the sense identified by Taylor there is no doubt that we are moral agents: we seem unable to exist without wondering whether this is good, that is the right thing to do, this unjust, that just wrong, and so on. And we are probably unable to exist without attributing, at least in unselfconscious moments, some kind of absolute value to our judgments: people, we insist, should never behave like that. But here the problems begin: we may be just tempted to make such judgments. These apparently absolute judgments may be typically human, but they may also be typically fallacious, representing not so much what is the case as what we should like to be the case. And, the argument would run, it would then be the task of the philosopher, if he wanted that to be his task (the conditional, however, is now im-

portant), to expose these errors and delusions for
what they are.[5] That, we would suppose, would be
his task if he were a lover of truth.

It is not easy to see what a philosopher (as distinct
from a sophist or a propagandist) could be if in some
sense he were not a lover of truth, though we shall
return to some postmodern difficulties with truth
later. From this point of view it does not matter if
truth is unobtainable; it would still be the
philosopher's task to reveal as much of it as possible
and to indicate the limits of its possible recovery
and presentation. So, it would seem that granted
that we apparently live in some kind of moral
space—that is, that we cannot avoid thinking that
in some sense or other there is a right and a wrong,
a good and a bad—it is the job of the moral philosopher to try to get behind these apparently obvious notions. And perhaps we can go a little further,
raising another possibility which may also depend
on an endemic and natural human error, but which
is at least worth investigating: that is the possibility
that there is some *difference* between saying that this
is right and that this is useful or that this is good
and that is pleasant. Clearly we at least think we
mean something different when we say that it is right
to punish mass murderers and that it is useful to
punish mass murderers. And it seems to be different to say that it is wrong to punish mass murderers
and that is useless to punish mass murderers.

It is easy to identify some of the foundational problems in ethics, even if they eventually turn out to be
somehow pseudo-problems. It is more difficult to
resolve them, and the philosopher, of course, is com-

mitted to resolving them by the use of his intelligence. That very fact, however, may set us off in a useful direction. Since it is somehow incumbent on us as philosophers to use our minds, perhaps we can approach the question of why this is right or wrong, good or bad, by arguing that this is rational, this makes sense, while that does not. By adopting such an approach we are not committing ourselves to believe that all there is to morality is rationality—even if that were to turn out to be the case; what we are committing ourselves to—and in this we are in the path of moral philosophers since Socrates—is the possibility that to do the right thing somehow makes sense, that it is the rational and reasonable thing to do.

To say that the moral just is the rational is to raise a host of difficulties, some of which we have touched on already. Let us, however, rehearse a few of them: that we lack the data to sort out the foundations (or even the applications) of morality; that even if we had the data, our minds are not capable of doing the job. Now such incapacity could be of two kinds, either or both of which may be the case. Our minds may be naturally inadequate for the job, or they may be deformed by the circumstances of our lives and of our cultures, so that we find it is extremely difficult to think rationally about moral issues when they touch us personally; or again it may be the case that our society is of such a sort that to know what to do in the abstract is at times impossible, at least in the sense that we will constantly be confronted with choices neither of which we want to make and both of which—it is indeed true—it would be better not to have to make. Augustine seems to have had such situations in mind when writing the nineteenth book of the *City of God* and speaking of this "darkness of social life," from which it would be delightful to fly away on the wings of a dove.

Or the problem may be less with the intellect *in abstracto* than in the will. We may not be capable of *wanting* to see the right answers in ethics, whether fundamental or applied; it would be too demanding to have to change our way of life. Or perhaps there is something in the Humean claim that our unaided reason at least is only instrumental; it can identify the means to moral ends without being able to justify those specific ends, or to identify the proper nature of morality itself. The only answer to this might seem to be to say that morality is merely being as rational as possible.

But that weakened claim—and perhaps even the stronger version—is itself open to several objections. One might ask why, in our thus weakened rational state, we are able to be so confident that by our unaided reason we are even able to identify the nature and claims of morality; or we might wonder whether we have any reason to suppose that we are under any obligation to be rational even if we have the opportunity to be so. If to that we merely reply that it pays to be rational, then morality is ultimately not a matter of rationality but of convenience. And that certainly does not explain the kind of horror we feel when we read of brutalities committed which are not inconvenient for ourselves—unless perhaps the mere hearing of them is unpleasant—and indeed have extremely little, perhaps virtually no, possibility of impinging on our ordinary lives.

Perhaps we may say that most of these objections to the *mere* identification of morality as rational behaviour boil down to just two basic points. The first is that whatever the importance or usefulness of rational behaviour, at least at times, we have no reason to suppose that rationality is the most important, and therefore the definitive, feature of human behaviour: in other words rationality may be a good, but it may not be the highest good. Perhaps it is worth pointing out that if certain religions, including Christianity, were to be telling the truth, rationality, though an important attribute of God, and therefore of man in his image, is not the only or even the most important such attribute.

A related religious question cannot now be evaded—both because of its immediate relevance at this point of the argument, and because it will come up later when we are considering the relationship between secular and Christian moral thinkers and what should be the nature of the dialogue between them. The point is simply that were Christianity to be true then both our minds and our wills *are* sufficiently weakened as to be unable to attain to certain truths without divine assistance, and hence that if we prescind from any reference to that assistance in discussions with our secular colleagues, we shall give away so much of our position in advance that it will be difficult to develop any kind of traditional Christian morality at all. We shall then find ourselves—and many of us do in fact so find ourselves—either producing a morality without foundations and to all intents and purposes purely secular, or compelled to smuggle in Christian articles of belief either at random or under some Kantian guise. But we shall return to such matters at a later stage.

Let us grant, however, at least for the sake of argument, what our previous argument has suggested should not be granted, namely, that we are all capable, by our natural powers, of usefully debating the first principles of ethics in some sort of reasonable expectation that our debates will be fairly successful. Perhaps if we are Christians we can reassure ourselves by some kind of natural law notion that (even in spite of the Fall) our rational capacities are still able to recognize the law written on our hearts— and not merely to recognize it, but—much more important philosophically—to justify it. For it is one thing to be able to know the right thing to do (even if we have not the strength actually to do it) and quite another to be able to explain why what is "intuitively," "obviously" (etc.) right is in fact right. I suspect that a lot of people (perhaps including the late Pope Paul VI) think that contraception is wrong without knowing any knock-down argument to show that it is wrong. But it may still be wrong— and it is certainly plausible that its intrinsic wrongness is not demonstrable (or even unintelligible) to non-theists.

Let us consider the claim that the first principles of morality may be available to our philosophical minds whether we are Christians or atheists (in good faith, of course). Note that we are not talking about the possibility that atheists can come to see that such first principles exist—for that might involve their also coming to see that God exists; we are talking about the possibility of useful arguments between theists and atheists in which both parties maintain their theological stance while at the same time reaching agreement—not, I must repeat again, about certain specific acts which must be done in some specific circumstance, like restraining a would-be murderer in a University classroom—but about the most basic principles on which such down-the-road decisions must ultimately find their rational and defensible justification.

What then does our question mean? It seems to mean something like, Does it make any difference at all in ethics whether God exists or not? That is not yet even a question about whether it makes any difference in ethics *what kind* of God exists, but does the existence of God in and of itself make any difference at all? Yet perhaps I have now made an improper distinction. Perhaps there are some kinds of gods whose existence or non-existence makes no difference at all to a possible thesis about the origin and first principles of morality. Perhaps the gods of Epicurus were of this sort. Epicurus himself thought that they did, in fact, make a difference, but perhaps he was wrong about that. What kind of difference did he think their existence made?

In antiquity Epicurus is the typical atheist, because, like Aristotle, but more unambiguously, his gods had no interest in human beings: he denied, in other terms, the existence of providence and any system of divine rewards and punishments. He is regularly hailed as a saviour of mankind precisely because he could show, they said, that we are annihilated at death and have therefore nothing to fear after our departure. It is interesting to note that what precisely often seems to modern man to be the great dread—the annihilation of the self—seemed to many of the ancients a happy prospect. Even Socrates mentions it as such in the *Apology*. But though the gods of Epicurus are too happy to have any interest in the doings of men, they are in fact ethically useful in two ways. Primarily they afford examplars of contentment; we too can be unconcerned and thus minimize the pain we experience, noting that, if like the gods we could minimize it altogether, we should be supremely blessed. A subsidiary attraction is that it is pleasing and relaxing to take part in religious activities—provided you have no belief in their religious truth (or fear that you might have such belief). Epicurus himself was enrolled in a variety of mystery cults, and doubtless part of his satisfaction was derived from observing the folly of the believers; also, like some of our more modern religious aesthetes, he may have just liked the music.

So, in providing models of the happy life Epicurean gods have an ethical purpose, though that purpose is rather minimal. Provided one could swallow the rest of the reductionist account of the universe which Epicurus provides, to enjoy and be comforted by the behaviour of the gods is little more than an optional extra. So, the essential point in connection with the impact of theology on ethics seems to be not just the existence of the gods, but—precisely what Epicurus denied—the existence of Gods with certain moral (or at least demanding) ideas or characteristics, and the consequent existence of some kind of relationship between the gods and human activity. That interest need not, then, be a moral interest, but we need not concern ourselves with non-moral versions. In the contemporary world the debate between Christians and secularists is a debate in which the possible God in question is the source and guarantor of morality—in some sense— and deeply concerned with the rights and wrongs of human behaviour.

It would be far beyond my present concerns to consider the different types of what might be called providential deities in the contemporary world, though such a wide analysis would be required if our topic were to be treated exhaustively. But it is probably adequate for present purposes if we consider some at least of the less controversial and more traditional features of the God of the Christians, and that consideration will be linked with an enquiry into whether there are specially Christian virtues, or at least virtues which are essential or native to Christianity (and perhaps to other religions) but which cannot be squeezed out of non-theistic thinking—indeed which are often and rightly (from their point of view) condemned by secular thinkers as superstition (at least when such thinkers forget to exercise their prized virtue of tolerance).

Without going into historical details there is little doubt that Augustine, who took a rather fierce view of pagan "virtue," was already quite clear about the fact that believers in the Christian religion must propose an understanding of the virtues which is impossible for pagans: which indeed is only possible for those who believe in a God very close to the God of the Christians both in the sense that such a God must be viewed as a creator (and probably also as a redeemer) and in the sense that God must be seen as a God of love, love being considered an essential, perhaps even the most essential attribute. From such a belief, in Augustine's view, arise both the claim that love itself is the basis of the other virtues, which thus become, in his language, "nothing other than forms of the love of God" (*On the Life-Style of the Catholic Church*, 1.15.25) and the specifically Christian understanding of the virtue of humility, a virtue necessarily impossible in its Christian form for non-theists.

If love itself is the basis of all the other virtues, then Christian ethics must be—at its root—quite different from all the other types of theory at present on the moral philosophers' table. Christian love is much more than, though inclusive of, any Kantian notion, however defended—a point to which we shall have to return—of that respect for other persons which finds its formulation in the claim that we should always treat others as ends in themselves, not merely as means. This is so for at least two reasons: first because such a claim itself depends on the notion that the only good thing is a good will, and that a good (and autonomous) will is to be identified as a rational will—ultimately we are to act as we do because that is the rational, and hence autonomous thing to do. But acting out of a love of God cannot be merely reduced to choosing the rational course, even if that course *will turn out* to be the course in which we make no "moral" exceptions in our own interest.

Secondly, the love of God quite specifically demands the actual existence of God, whereas at least in theory the Kantian ideal of a being possessed of the required kind of right reason need not exist at all. Certainly Kant, who thinks that all human beings are radically flawed, cannot find an example of the moral life except in a God, though he claims himself that the only role God can play in ethics is to provide an assurance that the demands of morality are ultimately reconcilable with the longing for happiness—itself, of course, in his view, a longing with no moral content. Given the non-existence of God, Kantian ethics remains a non-realizable ideal, and the worrying question then immediately arises, why is it to be pursued? The answer, because it is the rational thing to do, is more than a little weakened if we also realize that it is beyond our power. If we are the kind of beings who are incapable of acting in perfect reason, why should we pretend that so to act is an overarching demand upon us? Why should we not conclude from the apparent non-existence of so-called moral beings that the notion of morality we are pursuing is the wrong one for the human race?

Again, perhaps we can say that we should be as rational as we can. That weaker proposal is open to additional objections. The supreme good is still rationality as such, but it does not exist, so why should it be taken seriously? If rationality is only a hypothetical good, why should we take it for a real good? The best answer to that—and something like it seems to be current among a number of contemporary moral thinkers—is that it is convenient in vari-

ous ways to assume such a moral ideal, even if it is
in fact unattainable. But this runs up against two
difficulties: on the one hand it seems to imply that
self-deception, and the deception of others, are necessary parts of the moral good,[6] while on the other
it suggests that there is something specially to be
denoted "moral" merely in what is supposed to be
convenient for some or all of us. That defence cannot be proposed by any kind of Kantian, lest his
Kantianism collapse into hedonism or consequentialism—and a consequentialism in which the good
to be somehow maximized remains unspecified except in so far as it is convenient.

Kant himself certainly subscribed to some version
of the doctrine of original sin, at least in so far as he
held that we are subject to a fundamental and inexplicable moral weakness, so it would at least be open
to him to supplement his account of the moral ideal
by saying that, although we are too weak to achieve
it, we could at least do so with God's assistance; that
move, of course, is not open to most contemporar-
ies who call themselves Kantians, who must either
deny human weakness—a move which in the recent twentieth-century at least looked more and
more implausible—or they can say that it is our
(comparatively ineffective) human reason which
"constructs" the good life: on the basis of the principle that the demand for the universalization of
moral judgments will in fact eliminate all candidates
for inclusion in the good and moral life which do
not in fact lead to the notion that human beings are
to be treated solely as ends and never merely as means
to further ends.

That still leaves a package of unanswered questions: above all why is such a life, merely because it is (if it is) the most rational life, necessarily the highest life—at the least it could well be incomplete, and most philosophers who believe it might lead to a world of strict justice but hardly of kindness, let alone of love, would say that it *is* incomplete; and secondly, even granted that such a life is claimed by some to be the highest life precisely because it is the nearest we can get to a rational life (and therefore a life free from the domination of the passions), why should we accept such an evaluation? In other words granted that this is the most rational life, and even the "freest" life in the sense of the most-self-determining life on at least a possible (if implausible) account of the self, still the question remains as to why we should follow it. Then it would be less rational to do otherwise, but it might still in some other sense be "better." The only answer to that would have to be (again) that we know that the best life for man is simply the most rational we can achieve or that it is that which is the most free. The latter assumption (and it is no more than that) entails that the option of being wholly self-determining is the best thing in the world—which in that sense Christians must deny, since they define freedom as the ability to recognize (with "outside" help) that the best thing is to love and obey God, recognizing our own inability to "go it alone." The former claim, as we have seen, that it is simply the best thing in the world to be as rational as we can, is also no more than that: a claim, an assumption. The only conclusion to be drawn from all this is that, unless the Christian is prepared to compromise his position before the argument has even begun, there is no reason to assume that he will be able to find common ground *at the base* of ethics on which to make common cause with Kantians either of a theistic or of a non-theistic sort.

If with Kantians the discovery of such common ground is unlikely, it is even more unlikely that those who want to argue that the best life depends on the love of God will be able to find common ground with consequentialists of a secular sort—who will necessarily have difficulties both in determining a reasonable account of what good is to be maximized once they pass beyond what can be roughly called material goods, or how this maximization, and its relevant decisions, can in fact be achieved. Probably there would be more success with religious consequentialists, if they want to argue that what should be "maximized" is the opportunity to accept and enjoy the love of God and to work accordingly. But although there remain difficulties with that they are not our immediate concern: that concern being with how it is possible to find common ground for the justification of ethics between people who think that there are reasons to believe in the existence of a loving and providential God and those who do not. Let us, however, repeat once more that this apparent difficulty of justifying the first principles of morality in no way precludes agreement between the two parties on specific moral questions, and indeed if the secular party wishes to rely on some version of the "as if" morality, where moral norms are treated *as if* they are objective, or on some form of ethical paternalism (including what Bernard Williams once dubbed "Government House" Consequentialism[7]), we will be able to discover an apparent, though not a real agreement about how to justify moral behaviour in general—but at the price of deceiving those who are not members of that philosophical élite which is in the know.

We conclude, then, at least for the moment, that the Christian belief that there exists a loving God, and that the virtues must be related to that loving God, provides a serious barrier to any genuine agreement on the first principles of morality between theists and non-theists. That is an argument and a problem about the possible existence of God, a problem, that is, which arises outside the domain of morality as such but which necessarily affects what lies within that domain. Our second original question—whether there are any specifically Christian virtues which the pagan or secularist must deny as superstitions—though obviously also interlocked with the matter of the existence of God itself, is also related to the problem of the consequent nature of man.

Apart from crazy Sartrian ideas about our total freedom to make and remake our moral selves (though Christians have a plausible explanation as to what happens when such ideas are propounded), there is clearly a sense in which any intelligible ethical theory is naturalist and cannot be separated from what might look to be ethically neutral problems of the nature of man. Although "ought implies can" is sometimes false or at least seriously misleading in ethics—"or what's a heaven for": a heaven, that is,

which represents an ideal to strive for even if it is
unattainable, at least in the present life—it certainly
indicates an important truth: that is, that it is absurd to indicate moral goals (or physical goals) in
complete disregard of the kind of beings humans,
and indeed particular humans are. We do not expect athletes (at least without steroids[8]) to complete
a two-minute mile, or professors to cycle to work if
they have lost their legs. Nor should we expect su-
perhuman moral feats, works of supererogation,
from all and sundry; they are precisely works of supererogation in that we do not blame people for
not performing them.

We may assume without further ado that it is not
possible to detach any sane moral philosophy from
some theory of man, some account of human nature and of what is now called theory of action. But
it is important to see that this theory of man might
or might not have a supernatural dimension; at its
crudest that means that man might or might not be
created by God, and created by God for some purpose. Clearly our theory will have to be different
depending on whether man has been created by God
for a particular purpose or he has not been created
by God at all and thus has no particular purpose
beyond those which he chooses more or less rationally to adopt. Of course one could say that even if
man has been created by God, it is still possible to
argue to an ethical position without reference to that
creation and to whatever divine purpose man might
have, and perhaps this is how Christian moral philosophers, in their holy zeal to talk the same language as their secular counterparts, would have to

operate. Such an enterprise might provide a fallback position for Christians—they would know what to do if they lost their faith, then inhabiting the same world as their secular counterparts. But it must also be recognized that such an operation, if Christianity is true, is a futile exercise, for it could not produce an ethical theory which matched the nature of man as he actually is, only of man as he might be in some other possible world in which neither he nor it was created by God.

That being so, we have to recognize that our search for the nature of man, which must, as we have argued, be related to the form of ethical theory we can present, has to develop in not one but two directions: we need to consider the nature of man not only from a psychological, sociological and anthropological point of view, to determine (against any would-be Sartrians or their successors) what we are capable of doing through a series of empirical enquiries, but we must also conduct a more or less theological or atheological enquiry and propose certain rules from that sector in which we can consider what human beings are for or not for and capable of or not capable of. Let me offer a single but I think informative instance of one of the ways in which such an enquiry can shed light on apparently very common forms of ethical perplexity.

Every time we read or see on the screen some particularly barbarous or "unspeakable" atrocity, whether in the private domain—a pedofile has been caught torturing and enjoying torturing his victim—or in the public domain where we meet yet another mass murderer (Stalin, Hitler, Pinochet, Pol Pot, Idi

Amin, Saddam Hussein: the list is endless with no likelihood of the numbers going into decline), we read and probably express our emotions or thought in the form of a comment about its all being not just unspeakable but totally inexplicable, unimaginable; while philosophers like Harry Frankfurt make wise remarks (against, say, Hume)[9] about such outrageous behaviour with reference to Hume's comment that there is nothing irrational about preferring the destruction of the whole world to the scratching of one of his fingers, replying that such comments indicate that certain sorts of moral discourse are outside the range of rationality altogether, while offering little explanation of why this is the case.

But am I wanting to say that the behaviour of some genocidal tyrant or serial-killer is imaginable and quite intelligible? Well, Yes and No. It may be the case—I hope it is the case—that *we* cannot imagine ourselves as capable of such acts, that though some of us may be tempted to imagine what it would be like to murder, rape, or torture another human being, we are sickened at the very prospects of such acts, etc. But to generalize from what some human beings could play with in their imagination to what all human beings can imagine themselves actually doing is a false move. True, there are ways even for criminals of this sort to rationalize away their guilt and the nature of their actions. They can be "persuaded," and their cynical bosses will try at times to persuade them—in the process sometimes, as Plato pointed out, being so persuaded themselves—to think that their victims are not really humans at all.

Nazis made humans look like rats, pretended that they were rats, and certainly induced in many of their extremists (non-German almost as often as German, as membership lists of the SS make clear) the belief that they were a kind of vermin, and of course should then be treated as such.

But we should not be deceived too easily ourselves either. Mass murders are committed in part, but by no means entirely, because people are deceived and self-deceived about what they are doing in the crudest of ways. But only in part: they are often carried out, and indeed ordered, because with their eyes open people want to treat other people in those sorts of ways. Many men like torturing other men, history is a stark recorder of the fact, and they can buttress this satisfaction by all kinds of ideological justifications. But they do not always do that: mass murderers sometimes tell the more disturbing truth about themselves, Nazi Germany as often providing illuminating examples. Goering said he joined the NSDAP, not because of all the ideological stuff, in which he had no belief or interest, but because he was a revolutionary, a nihilist, a lover of destruction; von Roehm said it was because after a life of violence he could not settle down to something more bourgeois.

We should not be deceived, and on this sort of matter we can learn a lot from Augustine who was not deceived: people often do wrong—normally and, fortunately, in small matters—because they want to do wrong or because doing wrong makes you look big among your cronies. Another Nazi example: Hans Frank, the notorious Governor-Gen-

eral of Poland, was described by one of his biogra-
phers as "the imitation of a man of violence."[10] It
seems that people pursue vice because it is in some
sense our nature, as we at present experience it, to
pursue vice. It would probably have helped a bit
from the theoretical point of view if Aristotle had
said directly that not only is man an animal uniquely
capable of virtue but an animal uniquely (and of
course necessarily) capable of vice: man, that is, of
course, as we experience him, man, as Augustine
(following a tradition which goes back via Cicero in
fact to Aristotle himself) would put it, in his "*second* nature." But if man has a second nature, and it
looks as though, whatever we may want to say about
his theological explanations of that nature, Augustine was right about the empirical facts themselves,
then when we experience that "unimaginable horror" at the acts of mass-murderers and say that these
acts are "unthinkable," we are using the word "unthinkable," or at least we *should* be using the word
"unthinkable," in a very special way. If we mean that
in accord with the dictates of right reason it is hard
to see how anyone could propose and seek to justify
such acts, that is only theory, and a matter for test-
ing: it is Augustine's view, for what it is worth, that
there must be a level of unintelligibility about such
acts, and we might say, if we wanted to put on a
Christian hat, that they are unintelligible in the sense
that they are acts in conscious or suppressed revolt
against the very nature of Goodness, that is, of God,
an explanation which might have the advantage of
explaining both how we find them meaningless,
though not of course purposeless or unintentional,[11]

and why anti-Semitism (not to be confused with criticism of individual Jews or of Judaism), that is, an attack on a people who have clearly been given a place in God's particularist economy of the universe (In some sense of "could" Jesus could have been a Puerto-Rican or the brother-in-law of Mussolini, but in fact it was not so), is so curiously attractive and has provoked in the Holocaust such an extraordinary version of well-organized human vindictiveness, cruelty, and deception.

If there is thus a sense in which such acts are unimaginable, in another sense, for a Christian—at least for a Christian who has not abandoned his traditional beliefs in favour of a pragmatic and shortsighted optimism about the potentialities of human nature and the difficulties of improving that nature—they are, if not imaginable, at least somehow *explicable*: after all in terms of traditional theology it required the action of God himself, not of man at all, to open up the possibility of more optimistic outcomes. If there is an inherent and deep-seated irrationality about evil behaviour (however effectively it may be organized and rationalized), then it would be impossible for the good man to imagine doing it, though he would be able to expect it, and to explain its origin. But probably this "explanation" would have to be theological, which is what in its turn explains the currently common use of the idea that evil is "inexplicable" as well as "unimaginable." Speaking of the Second World War, a contemporary (and unbelieving) scholar remarked that it "defied the liberal imagination" and could only be accounted for by some "currently unfashionable theory

of . . . inbuilt, inherited corruption," that is, of a
primeval fall of mankind.[12] The difference between
such acts being "unimaginable" and their being "inexplicable" then would be that their nature, and in
particular their "origin," could be explained theologically whereas the resulting mentality cannot be
"imagined," because there are limits to the degree
we can put ourselves in other people's shoes: that is,
without in fact converting to their beliefs. But whatever the origin of ultra-evil beliefs—whether or not
consciously parasitic on God in so far as they want
to reject his existence not simply on ontological but
also on moral grounds—that sort of *explanation* of
their nature is perhaps available at least in part to
the believer and the non-believer alike. Both could
put them down to a human wish to be self-makers,
to be God to the degree to which they allow God to
be a logical possibility.

When it comes to their own actions, however, the
believer and the non-believer will differ in the sheer
stupidity of their behaviour, and perhaps (in the
believer's terms) in the moral disvalue of their
behaviour, in that the believer who behaves with
extreme brutality, even if he pretends to be an unbeliever, would be more stupid, in his own terms, as
well as more evil, than the unbeliever himself. He
would be not accepting God's existence, but attempting to cause the death of God.

Which brings us back to the case of a specific virtue—not just the overarching virtue of love—in
which the Christian virtue must in a sense be the
secular vice: vice that is, in particular, in that it would
represent an offence against truth. Of course, there

is no fundamental reason why truth for its own sake should be important to the secularist, though he would rarely want to admit that outside élite circles for fear that the general public would believe him and wish to exact a terrible revenge. No one likes being deliberately deceived even if one is happy to deceive others, unless under some posture of professionalism one may enjoy watching the skill of a highly paid master of his or her craft, as one might enjoy watching a dexterous conjurer or silicon-tipped striptease artiste. And perhaps in particular, as Augustine realized when he named his Milanese Chair of Rhetoric a Chair in Lying, no one wants to be deliberately deceived by a professor—and the professor of ethics in particular might need to argue that he is not in fact, though he could be (and actually is), a professional liar.

You have probably guessed by now that the theistic virtue I have especially in mind is the virtue of humility. To understand it, however, we must first of all rescue it from any possible confusion with mere self-abasement, and secondly explain why it is that such a confusion can easily arise, indeed has sometimes arisen in the course of the history of Christianity as of other religions: a confusion which can lead to the image of the humble man as either exhibiting a slave-mentality—the charge of Nietzsche —or of merely living out a type of dishonesty, such dishonesty arising from the supposed impossibility of living a genuinely humble life without recourse to false modesty and even to hypocrisy: the sort of charges which are regularly levelled against what are taken to be impossibly demanding lifestyles, as Hegel leveled them at those who would claim to live out the morality of Kant.

Humility, in the sense I want to understand it, and in perhaps the only morally useful sense of the word, is primarily a virtue whose excellence is strictly tied to the notion of truth. When Aristotle in his *Nicomachean Ethics* spoke of the virtue of a figure that is taken (at least by some) to represent an ideal precisely the opposite of the Christian notion of humility, he too spoke of truth. His great-souled man claims for himself no more and no less than he is worth. His standard of measure is other human beings, and he would be vicious not only in so far as he claimed more than his desserts but in so far as he claimed less. Such ideas therefore bring in the notion of truth; if it is wrong for me to claim less than my worth, that is in part due to the fact that I am not insisting on my true value; I am dissembling, in the attempt to mislead either myself or others. But this is not the outright self-assertion which some have thought it to be, nor would the Greeks have supposed it to offend against the Delphic maxim that one should pursue nothing too much, that one should do nothing to excess.

In such consideration of the notion of the Aristotelian great-souled man, we can immediately recognize the difference from the Christian concept of the wise man as we have begun to represent it. In the first place, although we have pointed out that the Aristotelian and the Christian conceptions have in common a reference to the notion of truth, that is, to the correct and true moral condition and self-evaluation of the hero or otherwise in question, they

penetrate the secrets of the human heart: God, says Augustine, might in fact even save members of the acting profession (*To Simplicianus on Romans* 1.2.22)—at which point some of his readers, at least in antiquity, of course, might think to themselves: "And we all know how often *they* take their clothes off in public."

Be that as it may, the two attitudes are as follows, and here I am alas merely plagiarizing some remarks of my own elsewhere: on the one hand we are mere dust, and to dust we shall return—indeed in a sense we are less than that since the race itself, with some point, was created from *nothing*. And we can recognize how Christian and other religious writers are certainly fond enough of saying—in what sense is it self-*abasement*?—that we are as nothing and that God can do what he likes with the pots that he has made. (In one sense this may be a fairly simple problem about omnipotence, as, when I say that I'm not the kind of person to kill a beggar in the street, I do not mean that I have insufficient strength to pull the trigger.) The other side of the coin is that at least for a Christian such pot-language must be to some extent hyperbolical if it is also the case that we have been created by a loving God in his image and likeness—assuming, that is, that the likeness has not been entirely blotted out, in which case we are in trouble anyway about personal identity, because God would apparently have to create not a revised me but another me at the Resurrection. For to be in the image and likeness of God, even in so far as it entails being a living being, is a bit different from being a pot—a point which perhaps Hobbes did not see when he compared us with the famous "ship of Athens," apparently supposing that we seem to be the mere sum of our replaceable material components. But it makes sense to say that I am fat or that my body is fat; it makes no sense to say that my body is unjust.

In this particular case of pot-language it looks as though part of the truth of the matter would have to be that, at least from God's point of view, we cannot be just dust, though we may derive from that and presumably, if God—heaven help us—wished to change his mind (or should we say he always knew that he intended to change his mind, or something?), we could return to it permanently. When we say that we are like the pot in the hands of the potter—and religious people, not only Christians, I repeat, do say things like that—it may look like self-abasement, but it should not be taken to represent self-humiliation (rather than humility) when looked at precisely from God's point of view.

At any rate, whatever the appropriate attitude we may adopt in the face of our dependent situation, it must be clear that we are called on both to recognize that we are created and dependent and at the same time to recognize what we are created and called on to be, namely, the image and likeness of God. To adopt the proper attitude to our dependence, therefore, whatever precisely that attitude would be—certainly it would involve a foreswearing of any claims to be self-creators; indeed such claims would be the exact opposite of what would be appropriate—would be unambiguously a virtue. So, we should here have identified both a specifically Christian virtue and an attitude which could only be designated superstitious in properly secular circles.

It cannot be denied, of course, that there could be some sort of secular analogue to the Christian virtue of humility, a virtue by which, once again, we could recognize the limits of our importance, our talents, and our claims on others, but the fact of the absence of God in such contexts is crucial. The secular virtue could not be the same virtue, nor within the relevant scheme of things could it have anything like the same importance, as its Christian counterpart.

Quite apart from the problem of the overarching role of love within a Christian ethics, the existence of specifically Christian virtues, not to be recognized as such by secular philosophers, will probably also affect the nature of those virtues apparently valued in common by Christians and secularists: if not their nature, at least their application. Let us therefore briefly consider some difficulties with one of the most important of these virtues, that virtue of impersonal justice which seems to lie at the root of much secular theorizing and which must certainly find its proper place within the alternative Christian schema. Christians will have to admit that impersonal justice must find its proper place within a proper social and political system, but the nature of that place will almost certainly differ from the pagan or secularist ideal. First of all, even granting (for the sake of argument) that impersonal justice is not only rational but also desirable and to be imposed within the best society, both the overall dimension

of Christian love and the fact of man's dependence
on God and his consequent humility will affect the
way that impersonal justice is turned into legisla-
tive and political fact. Impersonal justice involves
treating all members of a society in a similar manner with respect to certain specific offences and op-
portunities within that society. It demands that the
weak and the powerful be held equally responsible
for their actions; that bribery, influence-peddling
etc., be excluded from the internal relationships of
the society, etc. But in many areas of ordinary life,
for example, in the matter of sentencing, the Christian will have constraints on his behaviour which
the secularist will not or should not allow. The Christian will recognize the frailty of the human race in
general, the difficulty of avoiding temptation, and
so on, precisely in the light of his account specifically of original sin and ultimately of evildoing seen
in terms of a rejection of God's grace. While recognizing, that is, that within a secular and temporal
context crimes need to be punished impartially—
there must be toughness without undue or vengeful
savagery—he will also refuse to condemn the sin-
ner to the extent that he will allow both that only
God can read his mind—both in respect of his reasons for crime and of his possible repentance—and
that it ill becomes us to vaunt ourselves on our own
moral superiority (but rather give the credit to
God)—at least if we take seriously the challenge of
Jesus about the person fit to cast the first stone.
Without a recognition of the importance of the place
and role of God's existence in any formulation of a
properly Christian morality, it will be hard for the

secularist even to comprehend the Christian attitudes to such apparently agreed virtues as impersonal justice.

*

We seem to have established thus far that the existence of God makes a difference both to the nature of the virtues in general and individually, as understood in a Christian framework, and to the very existence of at least one primary virtue as a special instance. The natural inference from this is that debate about the first principles of morality between theists and non-theists (and specifically Christians) would be unable to reach common first principles in essential areas of moral life unless one side or the other makes or slips into fairly drastic compromises about the actual content of its proposed moral vision. That would seem to suggest that we are at an impasse if we are hoping to secure agreements in honest debate rather than win a phoney war with an antagonist of straw. And it is surely odd to claim that the art of philosophy, even the art of ethics, is to develop the skill to trick an opponent into giving up his basic positions unnecessarily—or merely so that the argument can proceed—or to learn how to talk past him in the hope of convincing, if not him, at least some apparently interested third party that genuine progress is being made.

Perhaps the solution is to muddle along: we do not need to bother about foundations; men and women of good will and a commitment to the philosophical endeavour will make progress. Indeed they are doing so already. Look at the flourishing state of our philosophy departments; we have thousands of more or less satisfied students, etc., etc. Rawls, in a recent book,[13] seems to think this is a satisfactory approach, and I have heard various versions of it offered from time to time by a number of prominent philosophers, especially from the United States. It is, after all, a democratic move in some sense of the word "democratic." We can sit down together and by a process of compromise and hard bargaining hammer out a workable practical policy in ethics as in any other area of public policy.

In the light of our earlier discussion it must be apparent that I have little patience with, and little confidence in, such proposals. They seem to be yet another way, not of settling disputes, but of pretending that they do not exist or do not involve matters of urgent importance. But this itself is a whole ethical agenda. Interestingly enough, there are again analogues in certain kinds of theological debate, when apparently agreement is difficult if not impossible to achieve. In theology, though such dealings may have the advantage of allowing each side to recognize that their opponents (or at least some of them) are not diabolically driven monsters, their theoretical results will smack of the lowest common denominator, probably slanted in the direction of whatever extra-theological theory happens to be the fashion of the day. The introduction and influence of rights-talk in debate about whether Christian priests can be female would be an example of the phenomenon. In that debate, once the relevance of rights-talk has been admitted, the original question abut women priests has already been half-begged.

That half-begging derives directly from the introduction of an apparently attractive and fashionable
but arguably irrelevant and mischievous set of considerations.

Our ethical parallel to this relates to the introduction of a claim that we can at least agree to leave
foundationalist issues untouched and hammer out
important agreements about apparently simple matters where we seem to find common ground. The
objection is that in accepting that sort of suggestion
we have given up so much that, if we can find agreement, we have done so at the price of self-deception, and—I should repeat—that is true even if we
reach agreement on a particular practical policy to
be adopted in a particularly demanding, even hor-
rifying, set of circumstances.

E. God and Agent-Relative Ethics

But surely, as we have said, both sides can at least
agree to start with human nature. Even here there
are hidden difficulties. A broad measure of agreement can probably be reached at the descriptive level,
or even at the level of generality at which, as we said
earlier, we recognize that we all somehow and ines-
capably live in moral space. But that agreement may
be misleading. Clearly it would be important to
know whether teleological considerations should be
invoked. If we are created by God, and God has a
certain purpose in his creative activity, our capacities, which may be recognized purely descriptively,
can also be arranged hierarchically, in order of importance. Not that we can necessarily so arrange

them correctly, but we have certain possible guidelines for attempting to do so. Our nature really is different if it has a teleological dimension, if we (or in older language our souls) are *intended* to be concerned to flourish.

One way in which that can be appreciated is by a consideration of the nature of wrongful or immoral acts. Assuming that such acts can be justified as such in a secular universe, they must be justified in a different fashion, and the justification must lack a very important dimension. If God exists and is providential, then wrongful acts—in addition to being wrong in some manner recognizable by a secular analysis, are—to put it crudely—the acts of a damned fool.[14] In view of God's plan, and the fact that our nature has been planned by God, to act wrongly is to act in a way in which we are bound to pervert ourselves, certainly spiritually and possibly also physically—or at least chemically. Immoral activity is thus, in either the long run or the short—or in both—necessarily self-damaging, even self-destructive.

Of course we may be told that concern for one's own happiness, flourishing or well-being has nothing to do with morality as such, even if it is not immoral to take it into consideration, but in the event of God's having designed us to become beings of a certain sort, then to disobey that divine plan is not only to disobey God who has told us to look to our own well-being—which thus should be of great concern to us—but to damage ourselves *blindly*, and thus in effect to mar our happiness by attempting the impossible, by attempting, that is, to become what we are not constructed to become. In a Christian frame of reference any strict separation between happiness and morality is out of the question in so far as the tradition teaches that God wishes all men to be saved, that is, *inter alia*, to flourish according to the best capacities which we possess. The truth of the matter is presumably that happiness, like at least most pleasures, should be pursued "by indirection."

Theists well before Christ seem to have recognised most of this. Our present subject is in effect the nature and origins of what is called agent-relative morality: the view, that is, that it is an essential part of virtue not merely to promote the good end but to have no direct personal part in promoting the bad, lest it damage the soul. The life of Socrates, as depicted by Plato and others, bears this out. Witness the story that at the end of the Peloponnesian War when the Athenian democracy had been defeated and the city was being ruled by an oligarchic junta backed by foreign troops, it was the policy of the rulers—as it often is in such cases—to implicate as many prominent citizens as possible, not least those with a reputation for virtue, in their crimes. Though part of the reason for this, as we have already noted, is that corrupt people really like corrupting others, a further and more immediate attraction lies in ensuring that more and more of the citizens feel that if the government falls, they, as partakers in its iniquities, will be in trouble along with the bosses.

So, Socrates and three others were ordered to go to Salamis and arrest a certain Leon, who was then to be brought back to Athens and murdered for his money. According to Plato the other three went off to Salamis to make the arrest while Socrates went off home. The point is of special interest in that Socrates' action could not have saved the unfortunate Leon, who would have been—and was—murdered in any case. Plenty of others could have been constrained into doing the job had Socrates' defection made this necessary. But Socrates, knowing he could not prevent the crime being committed, took the view that it was not going to be committed through him.

Why would he take such a view? Precisely because he thought that his own soul would be damaged if he took part. Doubtless he could have given any number of reasons: that it was just wrong to do such things, that Leon was innocent or at least not proven guilty. Doubtless he might have considered all these points. But he also considered, and Plato, as a theist, certainly thought he was right to consider such things, that he should look after his own soul as far as he could. Not to look after himself, to damage himself, would be to do something which a man is not supposed to do. Or as Plato would have put it later on, acts of this kind, acts which involve a neglect of the good of one's soul, are not only harmful to others, not only hateful to the gods, but fail to take into account that we are in some sense supposed to look after our best interests.

Similar attitudes can be seen if we consider Socrates' attitude to suicide as Plato presents it in the *Phaedo*. We are like soldiers who have been posted as a guard; we cannot desert our post. We may believe, as does the Socrates of the *Phaedo*, in a very dualistic (and unsatisfactory) account of the soul-body relationship, and one which Plato considerably modified later, and consequently wish to be rid of the body, that is, to experience the separation of the body from the soul, but we are not allowed to anticipate that separation. We are intended to live in a certain way in this life, and even if the condition of this life is far from ideal, we must abide by the rules under which we live so long as the gods require us to do so. We are not our own masters; it is not we who have decided what is the best way to treat our souls. We do not invent morality; we discover it, and in its discovery it may turn out to be unexpectedly difficult and even unpleasant in the short term. We conclude that such an interpretation of agent-relative morality is certainly theistic, but not necessarily Christian, though it is necessarily subsumed into Christian ethics. If we are created in the image and likeness of God, it is in *God's* image and likeness that we have been created, and no consideration of what can be determined by reason alone—unaided, that is, by God's revelation of his own nature and desires—can take that adequately into account.

There is a certain type of ingenious move, deriving from earlier historical debates in Christian theology, which is sometimes invoked by Christian philosophers to get us out of difficulties of this sort. It is claimed that by reason alone and only quite indirectly guided, we can discover our natural end, but over and above this we have a supernatural end. In so far as concerns our natural end, the argument then runs, we can debate and find substantial common ground with the secular thinkers. To consider this move we need both to glance briefly at the origin of the debate about natural and supernatural ends, and to see why the distinction is of little help in our present difficulties; indeed how it can become yet another way in which the religious thinker is induced to give away his position before the argument has even begun.

Some at least of the origin of the debate about natural and supernatural ends is to be found in the attempt in the Middle Ages to assimilate into Christian theology the account (or possibly accounts) of the best life for man to be found in the *Ethics* of Aristotle. According to Aristotle the superior life for man is the life of contemplation, the second best is the life of virtuous activity in the *polis*. The first is the life of God, its difficulty therefore being that we can only attain it briefly, and perhaps some of us cannot attain it at all. But (luckily for contemporary scholars who have thus developed a cosy cottage-industry) Aristotle never spells out the relationship, if any, between the two lives, nor does he make clear what might happen, and what action should be taken, if the demands of the two lives seem to clash within a single individual.

I do not think that Aristotelian answers to these difficulties cannot be found, but that is not our present concern. What matters now is that when the scholastics and others were confronted with such texts the idea arose—again I do not want to get into the details—that perhaps Aristotle's life of moral virtue could be Christianized as the "natural" life, the life outside a specifically Christian framework. As such there would then be a natural end for man—and that end could be identified and (later on) debated with secular philosophers, prescinding from any specifically Christian claims. The nature of the "moral" life would thus be debated by trained reason, with no ground which could not be shared with all interested parties, but if one wished—when writing an ethics book—one could introduce certain more specifically Christian or at least theistic claims, like icing on the cake—perhaps sketching a certain foundationalist justification of the "right answer"—in some final last chapter, after the debate with and within secular philosophy has been "won."[15]

Apart from the oddity, to which we have already alluded, that in such debates the secularists seem never to be impressed—while the non-secularist is tempted to abandon his special claims in advance for such a meagre result—the whole application in such a way of the distinction between natural and supernatural ends—whether so used by Aquinas or not[16]— is unsatisfactory. For the issue of fact is whether man has a supernatural end or not. If he does, then any attempt to identify a purely natural end for him smacks of unreality, since there is no being for whom this natural end alone is appropriate. Had God wished to create men with a natural end, he could have done so; if he has created him with a supernatural end, then that supernatural end must at every stage transform and transmute the natural end. Perhaps an example of this is to be found in the way in which we saw Augustine claiming that all the virtues are modes of the love of God. Clearly, if there were no God, man's natural end would have nothing to do with such love, and perhaps something more like the Stoic or Kantian view would be plausible. Virtue would then be something different from what it in fact is in any plausibly Christian view.

Given the existence of God and of man's created being, it would seem therefore that man's natural end is a conceptual structure; there are no people who actually have or could have, in the present dispensation, such an end. But perhaps the distinction still has a use as a kind of thought experiment; perhaps it would enable us to talk usefully about morals with secular philosophers. There could be some truth in that, but the results which would come out of such debate would have to be negative. In so far as the natural end, in some such circumstance, would have to be largely what we can determine to be an end without reference to the activity of the Christian God (but perhaps not of some other divine being) as planner, it would fall under very similar constraints as those we have noticed already in debates between theists and secularists. The ensuing debate would thus have to be conducted in secular terms, and though *possible* moral structures could be produced and these structures could be coherent, there would be no guarantee that they would be true or worthy of our assent. A possible world is not an actual world.

From the theological point of view, however, it is important to record that a coherent and intelligible structure might be reached. That is because it is in accord with traditional theology that, although unaided reason cannot gain access to certain theological truths, yet when those truths are made available, they would be made available as intelligible. The problem that theists have encountered in their arguments with secularizers is not that they cannot come up with a possibly coherent structure, but that, given other possible kinds of secular or non-secular premiss, other equally coherent moral structures can be formed, and there is no means of deciding between all these structures except in terms of some explanation or justification of the premisses themselves. But it is precisely the possibility of theological premisses which is in question between the two groups.

F. Non-Religious Ethics

In the event of disagreement about the existence of God, disagreement in ethics, we have argued, should occur about the virtues, the goals of human life and more broadly about the nature of man. Thus in some respects, though not, as we shall see, in all, debate between secular and theological moral philosophers must be fruitless. Of course, we have assumed that secular ethics has been purged of all hidden "religious" survivals[17]—a necessity for genuine debate (rather than horse-trading à la Rawls or mere deception) just as much as is the purging from theistic positions of any inclination to abandon the necessary foundations and implications of such positions. A prominent secular moral philosopher, Derek Parfit, has been not only optimistic but unusually clear-headed about the present situation in secular ethics, and the unprecedentedly novel nature of that situation. He is therefore worth quoting at some length:

> How many people have made Non-Religious Ethics their life's work? Before the recent past, very few. In most civilizations, most people have believed in the existence of a God, or of several gods. A large minority were in fact Atheists, whatever they pretended. But, before the recent past, very few Atheists made Ethics their life's work. . . . Hume was an Atheist who made Ethics part of his life's work. Sidgwick was another. . . . Non-Religious Ethics has been systematically studied, by many people, only since about 1960. Compared with the other sciences, Non-Religious Ethics is the youngest and the least advanced. . . . . Belief in God, or in many gods, prevented the free development of moral reasoning. Disbelief in God, openly admitted by a majority, is a very recent event, not yet completed. Because this event is so recent, Non-Religious Ethics is at a very early stage. We cannot yet predict whether, as in Mathematics, we will all reach agreement. Since we cannot know how Ethics will develop, it is not irrational to have high hopes.[18]

Parfit's bold claims are not entirely accurately expressed. It is not true that atheism is as widespread as he suggests, except perhaps in some parts of Europe, of which Great Britain is one, but it is certainly true that many Western *élites* are now atheist, and it is among such *élites* that much of what I have described as secular thinking is carried on. What is interesting, however, and largely correct about Parfit's remarks is that he realizes that the study of ethics from an atheist (or even strictly agnostic) point of view must be a very different activity, and must lead to very different conclusions from those of traditional Western moral philosophers, most of whom have been if not explicitly, at least implicitly, religious in their assumptions. It is important to notice how true this is even among those who suggest, at times, that ethics can and should be separated from religious or metaphysical considerations.

I should explain that I want to use the term "religious" in a rather wide and special sense, perhaps different in two respects from that of conventional usage. I assume religious belief to be belief in the existence of some kind of transcendent being or reality which normally takes a moral or providential interest in our affairs. Perhaps the providence is not essential (but only the transcendence), but since theists are normally providentialists, I have hardly considered non-providentialists, such as Epicureans. (In fact, even for them, as we saw, the existence of some sort of transcendental reality is helpful in that it provides a model and standard for human behaviour.) We should notice that in an account of the varieties of atheism in the *Laws*, Plato may be right to indicate that both denial of the existence of gods and denial of providence have significant ethical repercussions. In antiquity, those like Aristotle and Epicurus who believed in a non-providential divinity or divinities were classed as atheists.

Is even transcendentalism necessary? Would some kind of pantheism suffice? Probably not if coherently proposed, since pace the Stoics and others, providentialism and pantheism are probably incompatible, or rather the providence and morality of pantheistic gods are normally secured by the slipping in of certain more transcendentalist features and attributes.

Parfit is right in at least implying that before the widespread arrival of what he calls Non-Religious Ethics in the latter part of the twentieth century, there were very few ethicists of the sort he describes and desires. Aristotle and Kant, for example, would not fill the bill. Though Aristotle proposes an amoral divinity who is uninterested in human affairs, he relies on a notion of "the fine" as an ideal—but not a construct or projection of the human mind. This "fine" represents the highest goal of human actions, which are thus performed "for the sake of the fine." In such a position a certain hidden transcendentalism, probably of a Platonic type to which Aristotle is not strictly entitled,[19] is obvious.

Similarly Kant, who wants to separate ethics from all metaphysical reasoning, ultimately needs a God who will guarantee the compatibility and reconcilability of our longing for happiness with the performance of our proper duties and obligations. Similarly again—an example to which we have alluded already—much atheist rights-talk depends on a *de facto* metaphysical status for a "right." In practical terms this is usually offered as a variety of the "natural law defence," such as to justify the Nuremberg war-crimes trials, but natural law involves a metaphysic and cannot function without one. As a recent moral philosopher has noted once again,[20] it was easy for Locke to talk about natural rights; he could say that they are distributed by God. But it is more difficult for those of us who want a large part of Locke's conclusions without accepting Locke's justifications for those conclusions.

Parfit certainly has a point in arguing that there is not much ethics which adopts a strictly atheist standpoint, and that the new science of non-religious ethics is in its infancy. Where he falls down, however, is in his failure to understand the practical difficulty of escaping from the religious standpoint—in my wider account of the notion of "religious." In *Reasons and Persons* he is especially concerned to argue for a much diminished account of the importance of personal identity; indeed he wishes to develop an account of ourselves—which he sees as the most effective alternative to the discredited notion that we are Cartesian egos (something which we might be, but in fact are not)[21]—whereby we are to be seen as successive selves, in a somewhat Humean manner, like a club which continues over time with a gradually changing membership. I do not wish now to develop objections to this position,[22] only to notice that even if Parfit's reconstruction of personal identity is correct, he offers a very curious argument in its favour. Rejecting the claim that the account of human nature and the self which he proposes is unpalatable, he says that he much prefers it because once convinced of its truth he finds himself less egotistical and more willing to think and act on behalf of others. His argument would appear to be that,

since he is himself less important than he thought
he was, he has more scope to recognize the equal
importance of others. An objection might be that,
if he recognizes that he is less important, he might
come to think of others as *even less* important.

In general, Parfit welcomes his own conclusions
about the significance of his own identity because
he thinks that, although a greater impersonality in
our reasons for action may seem threatening, it
would in fact often be better for everyone.[23] His
point is that, if we each develop a more impersonal
sense of justice, others could benefit from our in-
creased likelihood of avoiding self-indulgence or
making exceptions in our own favour. But apart from
the difficulty which we raised earlier of the uncer-
tain advantages of a general increase in the impersonality of our reasons for action, it seems very odd
for Parfit to claim as a merit of his own philosophical proposals that others will benefit, that he will be
less egocentric and more altruistic, in as much as he
seems to be working under the assumption that such
things are goods. This gives us the feeling that Parfit's
whole project is parasitic on the "theistic," in his
case specifically Christian, mentality from which the
New Ethics is supposed to be freeing itself, and from
which, in the absence of God, it certainly should
free itself, as Parfit himself has pointed out. The New
Ethics ought not to avail itself without argument of
quasi-foundational notions of the common good,
let alone of an identifiable Christian good or of al-
truism.

Parfit says that Classical Utilitarians ought to welcome his position, but one of the classic objections

to Classical Utilitarianism is precisely that, though it talks about maximizing goods, it has no built-in formula for determining what is the greatest good it wants to maximize. In other words, that all that can be argued, pace the Classical Utilitarians, is that we should maximize X, where X is a good, whatever content we actually attach to that X; that we should maximize whatever in fact turns out to be, or is claimed to be, good or the good.

It certainly looks as though Parfit has not been radical enough; he has made the mistake, both common among secular moralists and liable to delude their theistic opponents, of supposing that somehow moral philosophers are, or should be, decent people, or that we all know what it is to be a decent person. In one way this is another version of the general type of error which I dubbed in the case of Rawls the democratic or American error. We are all decent but puzzled people who can resolve moral dilemmas by getting together and thrashing it out. And to this I objected that we can only thrash it out if at least one side compromises its basic principles. But the case of Parfit indicates a further dimension of the problem. In assuming that it is an argument in his favour that his view will, or so he claims, make him more altruistic, Parfit not only assumes that we (as moral philosophers) will all be decent enough to recognize decency when we see it, but that we are licenced to avail ourselves of such recognitions. Yet this seems to be only another example of the assumption of a real good to which we have argued that we have no self-evident entitlement outside a theistic universe. In other words, in not being radical enough, Parfit would be subject to the criticism voiced by Mackie, when, in commenting how we all tend to assume objective moral goods, he rightly observes that, if this practice is in fact logically defective and indefensible, we need to offer what he has called an "error theory" to explain its prevalence.[24]

The philosophical crime Mackie is criticizing, and which Parfit seems to commit, is that of knowing that some activities (let us say genocide) are just wrong, that others just are right, and that it is justifiable to talk in a moral way, not merely as a matter of convenience or squeamishness, about one outcome's being better than another. In Parfit's case the idea in question is that it is better—and better for Parfit—to be more concerned with other people. Clearly, if this were an absolute claim, Mackie would charge it with projectionism: for whatever reasons Parfit favours being more altruistic, and he has elevated this desire into some sort of suggestion that such behaviour is good as such, in a moral sense.

Perhaps Parfit can defend himself and a number of others who subscribe to similar theories, but he certainly cannot defend all secular thinkers who fall foul of Mackie's strictures. In order to test that, we need to ask why, in the absence of any theory of objective goodness of a metaphysical, transcendental or "theistic" sort (such as we have been considering), which would validate claims like, "Genocide is just wrong," the secularist is possibly justified in selecting one type of moral system rather than another. Here then are some possible answers to the question, Why in the world of Non-religious Ethics subscribe to one moral theory rather than another?

1. Because it is true and I, as a rational agent, am therefore able to recognize its claims. To which the traditional reply is: even if it is true, why are you obliged to follow it, rather than merely recognize its truth? Why can you not satisfy your reason and then choose to do something different, following another kind of truth, namely that you prefer to do something different?

But 1*: I can add that, though I have certain rational powers, I have many other powers as well, and though I may be able to give no compelling first-order reason why I should follow those powers even though such following would seem contrary to reason, I may still be entitled to follow them: either because I think that my reason is merely instrumental and cannot (and should not) determine its own goals, or because it can give me no reason why I should not *at times* act irrationally, or because it is in any case so inadequate that I cannot rely on its best advice. Such inadequacy may be either a matter of my individual reason being feeble, or due to the fact that the powers of the human reason in general are quite insufficient to cope with a wide range of problems and questions. There is no reason why there should not be truths beyond the human capacity to understand.

2. My second reason for following one theory rather than another is because it is coherent (or at least seems to be coherent). But coherence by itself does not guarantee correspondence with reality. It would do so if it included all relevant information, but there

is no guarantee that any moral system we could come up with would be complete in this way, and a great likelihood that it is incomplete.

3. My third answer might be, "Because I am a free and conscious agent." The objection to this is that we appear not to be free in many important respects, and even if we think we are acting freely we cannot know that we are. Thus in so far as this answer asserts that I can do, choose to do, and tell myself that I ought to do what I "want," it reduces to the claim—a reformed version of which is offered by Parfit—that I should follow my present aims.

This latter claim is much more interesting in that it is not question-begging. I may have certain sorts of aims and desires, and there seem to be no immediate and compelling reasons (other than those of prudence or convenience) why I should not follow them. But what if others refuse to do so? They must decide the same way as I do. Certainly I can give them advice on what I think of their behaviour, and my advice, with that of others, may affect their desires—it is certainly possible to learn to desire something, such as to hear a difficult piece of music, and to learn not to desire something, though habits being what they are, the latter is usually a more difficult process.

Parfit, in fact, claims that we should not simply follow our present aims, but our aims when submitted to critical analysis and reflection. In the absence of external standards (other than those of prudence and convenience, which our reason can take care of, at least up to a point), this seems a plausible procedure. It makes no unacceptable concessions to illicit "religious" considerations or metaphysical ideals; it starts with facts as far as we can determine them, namely, our present desires. It then submits these desires to rational checks; again a reasonable procedure, and no illicit "ought" is introduced. Reason will provide reasons why this or that desire should be followed or thwarted, but those reasons are only sensible advice. They need not, and should not, provide a list of duties or obligations. To a certain extent, however, they can check present desires not only for rationality but for their coherence as a set. What we decide to do when such checks are in place is another matter.

At any rate the advantage of a purified version of Parfit's non-religious ethic—purified, that is, of the remaining decencies which the religious ethics has left behind as something mandatory rather than merely optional—is that it provides a challenge to the secular thinker analogous to that which faces his religious counterpart. The challenge to the religious thinker is to engage in exposition and, if possible, debate with the secularist without giving away his principles, and without throwing his credibility away in advance; the challenge to the secularist is to produce a genuinely secular set of ethical proposals, with no indefensible "religious" and transcendentalist hangovers, and of course to insist that all law, convention, rights etc., are positive law. This may well turn out to be a challenge for the secularist as great as that which faces the theist: as we noted, the Nuremberg tribunals (and the rejection of positive law defences offered by the Nazis on trial) showed how much apparently secular activity has to depend on some notion of natural law of a kind which can only be fully justified in the framework of a theistic universe.[25]

G. Options for the Theist

We started off by considering the proper conditions in which a debate between secular and religious ethics could take place, and we asked what possible results might be expected. The prospect at this stage looks daunting. We have argued that at the level of foundationalism, little agreement is possible unless one side or the other abandons its principles, for good reasons or for bad. And we suggested that in our present post-Christian climate it is more usually the theist who abandons his: not, that is, that he is argued out of them, but that he abandons them as the price either of getting into an argument at all, or at least of making much progress in that argument. To this a discouraging corollary should probably be added. Since most moral debate takes place in a university setting, and the nature of that setting is dominated by secularist agendas, theists are at no small disadvantage. In addition to the fact that young students can easily pick up the idea, in their early undergraduate days, that the notion of a Christian philosopher is a contradiction in terms,[26] since much of the most sophisticated work in philosophy, as in other subjects, is done in an entirely secular setting, more advanced students are under pressure to conform to the secular norms, or at least to keep their heads down, until they are very well established in their careers, by which time temporizing may have become deeply ingrained: one of the forms such temporizing often takes in ethics has been indicated in the present discussion.

Is there nothing practical to be done? Fortunately, there certainly is, for retiring into a theistic ghetto is of little philosophical help. To see how and where cooperation with secular thinking has been and can be highly beneficial to secularist and theist alike, we need again to look back to Socrates, the founder of Western philosophical ethics. There is no doubt that in a certain sense Socrates was a traditionalist; he certainly seems to have had a good deal more sympathy with much pre-philosophical thinking than did his Sophistic rivals.

The reason why Socrates seemed (and seems) *un*traditional is to be found less in the kind of positions he advocated than in the fact that, unlike the traditionalists, he recognized the need to justify them. The Sophists, he realized, could not merely be denied; they had to be answered. And in the process of answering, a great deal of confusion had to be cleared away, and a great many pseudo-reasons and rationalizations for behaviour had to be abandoned. These pseudo-reasons, rationalizations, and sheer bad arguments often came from the traditionalist camp, and here Socrates was with the critics. But it is one thing to agree with a criticism, quite another to accept uncritically that the critic has the right constructive solutions to the problems. In fact—and Socrates certainly thought so—the proposed new solutions may in ethical respects be worse than the difficulties they are intended to solve. Heroic ethics may be crude and undefended; sophistic

ethics based on forced antitheses, for example, between nature and convention, may be simply immoral.

The modern theist can agree with Socrates that
substantial areas of unclarity remain even in working out what should follow from agreed premises:
the endless debates about the applications of the obviously useful theory of double effect are a good
example of this. But for many of us, doing the logic,
or the casuistry, is the least interesting part of ethics, essential though it undeniably is. What is much
more interesting and important are the premises,
and especially the hidden premises or assumptions.
It is in the identification of justifiable premises,
clearly laid out, that much of the fundamental work
of philosophy is done. That is in no small part a
work of the imagination, an ability to recognize an
illuminating parallel or analogy or to unmask a se-
cret but indefensible assumption. Here too the theist, always remaining careful about what he unwit-
tingly concedes and not forgetting to talk also with
his fellow theists—if you *always* think about something else, you forget what you once knew—can
work side by side with the secularist. There is nothing wrong, for example, in working side by side with
an old opponent in seeing how a particular thought
experiment, without any theistic premiss, will cash
out; it is worth investigating whether, and with what
further premisses, it might generate an argument or
set of arguments which are not only valid and possibly true, but actually or probably true. There is, in
other words, plenty of fruitful co-operation possible,
and there is no reason to suppose, as long as the

theist keeps his nerve, that he will not be as successful in identifying the dubious or false assumptions
of his colleagues as he is in recognizing flaws in his
own position.

To assist the theist in this kind of activity, it is
worth summarizing at least a few of the points of
which he should be aware. First, that the secularist
normally allows, and certainly should allow, that he
cannot offer a justification for exceptionless norms;
indeed that he should find the notion of an
exceptionless norm indefensible even if attractive and
if incorporated into some version of the "common
morality"—a morality, of course, deeply saturated
in transcendental Christianity and therefore off-lim-
its to the secularist unless independently defended.
The second point is that choice, when a good, cannot be separated from the things chosen. The theist
can agree with the secularist that choice is *important* in ethics, but he should find it hard to be convinced by his colleague that it is a *good* when de-
tached from its objects. Choice, of course, cannot
be considered in separation from freedom, and the
secularist and the theist should almost certainly also
disagree about the nature of real freedom. Obviously
the theist will be unable to convince the secularist
that freedom is identifiable with obedience to God
and the pursuit of the good.

H. Ethics and Metaphysics

It should not be difficult for those who know
something of the history of philosophy to identify
the place of the decisive turn in modern ethical en-

quiry: the turn which has produced the extraordinary difficulties in the way of direct and honest debate about the foundations of ethics. That turn was
made by Kant when, after being woken from his
dogmatic slumbers, he determined that theoretical
reason was essentially impotent, and certainly has
nothing to contribute to ethics. That, at its crudest,
is the root of modern theories of practical reasoning, constructivism, etc., which attempt to start from
considerations of human autonomy, whether identified with Kant himself as a state of the holy and
rational will or with Mill as the nature of the freely
determining agent.

Despite Kant's use of God to provide the ultimate
reconciliation between duty and happiness, his attempted banishment of transcendental metaphysics from ethics governs the secular modern scene,
and indeed necessitates it. If an alternative to that
scene is to be philosophically tenable, then a certain
type of metaphysics must return. Of course, the theist may merely reply, as in a sense Kant may wish
him to reply, that the assertion of religious truths is
adequate for simple, pietistic religion, and that it is
merely natural religion, metaphysical religion, which
is ruled out. The religious philosopher should not
welcome that sort of solution; he has no wish, as a
philosopher, to be a mere fideist, and in the Christian tradition it has long been held that, even if unaided reason cannot reach the nature of God, it can
certainly propose hypotheses which add up to a
philosophical understanding and justification of the
truths of faith: hypotheses, that is, which are philo-

sophically defensible if not strictly demonstrable in our present fallen state.

But reverting to the historical problem which we postponed earlier, we must argue that it is not any metaphysics which will do the job: obviously enough, since only a true metaphysics is a possible candidate. The theistic tradition of which some of us believe that Christianity is the developing fulfilment, started, as Augustine recognized, with Plato. It is not just any metaphysics which can provide an adequate philosophical framework for the truths of Christianity, but a Platonizing framework. Some Neoscholastics might want to deny this, but a very brief historical sketch of the relationship between Christianity and philosophy will show that they should not do so.

After recovering from their shock that the world was not about to end, that among the Gentiles it was not enough to explain how Christianity is the fulfilment of the Messianic prophecies of the Old Testament, that lengthy argument with the "world" was inevitable, and that within that world philosophers were among the principal opinion-formers and in a sense the principal intellectual and even religious opponents to be overcome, thoughtful Christians were forced to stake out their own positions in contemporary philosophical debate. Naturally, they clothed themselves in the ideas and expressed themselves in the language of whatever school seemed most appropriate to their needs, and of the prominent groups, the Sceptics and Epicureans, though useful in particular respects, were obviously unsatisfactory: which left the Aristotelians, the Stoics and

the Platonists. As we have already noticed, Aristotle
was thought of as an atheist, and in general his fol-
lowers in the Roman Imperial Age had an ill repute
as mere logic-choppers; Aristotelianism was only to
join mainstream Christian philosophy when it was
subsumed within an overall Platonism. Which left
the Stoics, supreme in the years before Christ, and
the various more or less avowedly Platonic schools
which were gradually asserting a dominance which
was to last until the twelfth century.

At first Stoicism seems to have been very attractive, both for its strict morality and perhaps especially (in the case of Tertullian) because its material-
ism (more precisely its vitalism) seemed to offer a
sound approach to the Resurrection of the body.
We should recall that it was a standard objection of
Stoics to Platonic accounts of the relationship between the soul and the body that such a relationship must be impossible unless the soul itself is a
material substance. Now it was a distinguishing mark
of Christianity, in contrast to various pagan wisdoms,
that it stressed not only the immortality of the soul
(though not its *natural* immortality) but also the
resurrection of the body. The Stoics, for their part,
could also easily accommodate their variety of ma-
terialism—because it involved a form of pantheism—with a material God, but for excellent reasons
the Christians learned, first in the East in the tradition of Origen, then in the West, that the transcendence of God which they required needs an immaterial divinity. Platonism, supplying both the
immaterialism and the transcendence, came by the
middle of the third century to replace Stoicism as

the most suitable way to convey the rapidly developing body of Christian theory. As Simplicianus put it to the young Augustine before his conversion, in the books of the Platonists are to be found an account of God and of his Logos (but not the Incarnation)—a combination which had appeared similarly attractive to the Jew Philo some three and a half centuries before.

It was above all the Platonist picture of God, as transcendent and as the source and nature of value, which appealed to the developing Christian thinkers, especially when coupled with a theory of the return of the soul through love to God. It is not my present concern to pursue that development except merely to note that Christian theologians were able to use the rich Aristotelian theories of man and of society, not least the Aristotelian theory of action, only when those theories were placed beneath the overarching authority of a transcendent God of Platonic origin—and viewed as a source of goodness, morality and providence far from the mind of Aristotle himself. We can now be certain that the supposedly Aristotelian God of Aquinas, as of Maimonides and Avicenna, is in essentials a Platonic divinity—though no "religiously motivated" product of the Middle Ages, but an inheritance from the Neoplatonized Aristotelianism of late antiquity.[27] In brief, we conclude that almost from the beginning of Christianity it has been a Platonizing conception of God which has best suited Christian theology; and there is no reason why that situation must not extend itself into the future. It is probably the case—there is at least empirical evidence—that not only is metaphysics necessary to give an intelligible account of Christian doctrine, but that that metaphysics must itself be theologically Platonic.

In view of the traditional and necessary relationship between most traditional ethics and the supposed existence of God, and in view of of the huge gap which we have identified between ethics within a theistic and metaphysical framework and the ethical mentalities dominant within contemporary societies, we revert to the question of where should the theist begin. Does it follow from my argument that, despite the common ground we have identified, unless the secularist can be induced to believe in the existence of God, there is no hope of his being persuaded into a satisfactory ethical position? If so, the situation looks hopeless in view of the notorious difficulty of persuading people to believe in God rather than of showing that God's existence is an intelligible possibility. Few atheists have been persuaded by sets of arguments to accept the existence of God; rather, as Newman put it in a related context, "the whole man moves," and he finds himself in another place.

What strategy should be recommended to the theist in the study of ethics? Probably it should be two-pronged. It should certainly include following up a set of insights which are now widely available. He must hammer home, by close analysis, the ultimately arbitrary nature of secular positions, recalling that, as MacIntyre has so strikingly pointed out,[28] contemporary debate in ethics, however sophisticated it appears on the surface, is little more than groups of partisans shouting slogans past one another. And there is no end in sight. That is the situation which has led to the desperate claims that we have no need of foundationalist theories and that we can get on well enough by sitting down and working out a reasonable and democratic compromise. But if that were all that could be done, we should still be near despair.

Fortunately there is a second option, and we have already seen certain indications in the present discussion of the path to be followed. What is required on the constructive side is a critical-historical analysis of the development of a foundationalist theory of ethics from its beginnings, and those beginnings, as we have seen, are with Plato. We could then show how Plato's first but decisive proposals, the postulation of a transcendent source of Goodness and an analysis of the human capacity to be inspired with love for that transcendent reality, have been refined over the centuries, especially in a Christian context, and most obviously by Augustine and his successors who have emphasized both God's omnipotence and man's moral weakness and inability to remain firm in his moral purposes: the theory of original sin. Then we should have to consider various attractive alternatives which have appeared to whittle away the theistic edifice that has been constructed, sometimes out of a misguided sense of Christian needs, sometimes out of a belief that a certain new philosophical path could have more fruitful results than it turned out to have in ethics. Such paths, in the scheme of things, have been by no means without reward, not only in the fruitful enlargement of ethical enquiry —as instanced, for example, by the new and proper attention to the personal individual and his autonomy which has acquired such importance since the time of Descartes—but also in the very investigation of those blind-alleys which with good reason looked to be more fruitful than they turned out to be. It is impossible to know whether a long blind alley is blind until one goes a fair way down it. But the difficulty then may be that one is too tired, too lazy, and too habituated to want to go back, let alone to admit that one has made a serious mistake.

In the course of such a critical-historical analysis, it would become clear what are the existence-conditions for a genuinely binding moral system, and the task of the analysts should then be to insist to the secularists that it is these conditions (including the existence of God) or nothing; that there is no intermediate and ultimately fudged position available to the genuine seeker after truth. The admitted chaos of modern ethics and the threat underlying the possibility that this chaos will become widely recognized in society at large would seem to give some encouragement that the task is by no means impossible.

Suppose moral philosophers become convinced that, unacceptable theistic alternatives aside, there is no hope for the establishment of ethical principles. They have then at least three options, and again we should not forget how dangerous these options are. The first is so to reduce the value and importance of human individuality, in the manner of Parfit, as to leave us looking all the more like the cogs in the machine which certain economists, geneticists, and car-salesmen would like us to appear. The second we have also considered; it is to look for a democratic consensus. The third, which might seem the more attractive after the threatened failure of the second, is to resort to systematic lying and deception, for the best consequentialist reasons. Many philosophers have been tempted in that direction, especially in more recent times. Politicians necessarily, if sometimes unwillingly, will encourage such temptations.

I. Lying in Philosophy

The basic attraction of philosophical lying is the belief that it is too dangerous for the ordinary public to know the truth. Sidgwick, as we have seen, inclined to this view, being concerned that, unless the public could accept a necessary relationship between happiness and morality they would choose against morality. And in any case it is worth reminding ourselves that lying is not necessarily a vice for a consequentialist, provided, let us say, it seems to be in the interest of the greatest number, and that we know what the interest of the greatest number adds up to. But what the consequentialist will not want to point out to the unsuspecting public is that even his philosophical statements, which they will naturally if naively take to be sincere attempts to reach the truth, may themselves reflect an economy with the truth designed to forward whatever is the philosopher's view, say, of the good of the greatest number. In other words, it is incumbent on the consequentialist to show, in a transparent manner which hardly admits of deception, why when he speaks, as he sees it, philosophically, he is also likely to be speaking not merely as cleverly but as truthfully as he can. Otherwise he might be concealing ethical truths in the interest, let us say, of persuading his hearers that, despite Sidgwick's mournful conclusion, duty and happiness are compatible after all.

It is also worth pointing out at this stage that I have not advanced anything which might seem an argument against all forms of lying and deception; what I have done is to suggest that it is particularly dangerous—in ordinary moral terms: terms, if you like, of the common morality—to lie about philosophical truths, unless you do not believe there is such a thing as objective truth in philosophy at all. (By this I do not mean to object to, say, non-cognitivism, for non-cognitivists claim that non-cognitivism is true, but to the much wider and probably self-defeating claim that there are no truths *in philosophy*.)

Once again, as we should now expect if the thrust of my argument is making any impact, we may see an interesting parallel between ethics and religion. Augustine was particularly rigorist in his attitude to lying, apparently viewing it as some form of blasphemy, but even within that rigorism, he was particularly severe, as his reply to a Spanish priest named Consentius makes abundantly clear, about lying in matters of religion, about lying in order apparently to advance the cause of right religion: it is peculiarly diabolical.

You may have noticed, however, that I prefaced my remarks about lying with the remark, "if there is such a thing as objective truth." So, before drawing some conclusions, I should add something more about objective truth, for it has an especial resonance in problems of contemporary ethics. We are said to be living in a post-modern age, and though no-one is very sure exactly what that means, one of its features seems to be a kind of philosophical perspectivism which goes back to Nietzsche, or at least to a reading of Nietzsche associated especially with Foucault. Nietzschean perspectivism or "genealogy" may seem to offer a more radical alternative to what I have called theistic ethics: more radical in that it denies and unmasks not only transcendentalism, but its whole range of modern alternatives (consequentialism, naturalism, Kantianism, contractarianism, and the others) with equal zest.

That means that my own position has something important in common with that of the post-Nietzscheans. We agree that the death of God entails (or would entail) the end of morality (as well as of any hope of finding a meaning in life). MacIntyre (in *After Virtue*) may have been right in arguing that when Nietzsche attacked "morality" he was thinking primarily of Kantian morality, but if Nietzsche's position were correct it would undermine any form of prescriptivity or normativity. That is not because the existence of God enables us to present God's will as the sole foundation of morality—there are good arguments against the notion that moral oughts are merely generated by God's will—but because the existence of God enables us to proclaim the exist-

ence of goodness, including moral goodness. Goodness, if commanded by God, would not be a matter
of arbitrary assertion, but a voicing by God of his
own nature and plan for mankind. Those who disobey God can thus only do so in a strict sense if
they also reject good actions in the knowledge that
they are objectively good.[29]

Part of the real challenge of Nietzscheanism is that
it forces us to acknowledge a radical dichotomy in
non-Nietzschean moral theory: morality either depends on God or it depends on the will and rationality of man. We either find it or invent it; it rests
either on fact or on choice. That does not mean we
invent its "natural" features. We do not invent the
fact that racking people is painful; we invent the
fact that it is also wrong. Of course, Nietzscheans
try to subvert both man-made and God-dependent
moralities, but that is not our present concern. What
is our concern is that we are agreeing with Nietzsche
when he asserts, in an adaption of the words of Ivan
Karamazov, that without God there is no reason why
we should not *decide*, some way or another, what is
right and wrong, thus leaving ourselves with the huge
difficulty of persuading others that they ought to
do what we, or some of us, or most of us, have decided (for whatever good reason) they ought to do.
In fact perspectivism gains much of its force, once
God is removed from the scene, from the fact that
we make our meta-ethical decisions about what is
right from some particular perspective. Without
God, much of the standard retort to relativism cannot be directed at a perspectivism which can be
loosely defined as relativism freed from its normal

dependence on non-relativist theories about human societies.

Where we have found common ground with the Nietzscheans is in the fact that without God there can be at least no objective *moral* truth. But human beings need to protect themselves against one another—note what happens when there is a police strike—and it has long been observed that doing what we "ought" because it is right has much more force—and therefore better promotes social cohesiveness—than doing what someone says we ought when we only recognize the "conventional" force of his commands and not the moral force. Or at least the force of law and convention is the stronger if it is buttressed by our belief that what law and convention proclaim to be right really is right. To go back to an earlier example, we are more impressed that genocide is wrong if we believe it is morally wrong than we would if it were merely illegal, like driving on the wrong side of the road.

So, if the Nietzscheans are right about the relationship between God and morality, and if they are also right that objective truth (at least in ethics) is a fiction formed through envy and the lust for power, then it is understandable that those philosophers who for whatever reason wish to maintain a stable social order would have even less repugnance than Sidgwick in advocating systematic lying and deception as a matter of public policy. Objective morality, they would know, does not exist, but it is better, from their perspective, if most people do not realize that. Hence let them be deluded—since truth for its own sake is of no concern to the new ethicist—

by those who can speak of morality *as if* it exists. Even without Nietzsche, and the Nietzschean features of post-modernism, such a solution, as we have seen, is alluring enough for the secularist. Given post-modern fashions and the complexities of contemporary life, its charms are almost irresistable.[30] Of course, one might suppose that just as democracy might have to tolerate everyone except non-democrats, so philosophy might have to tolerate everyone except liars. But whereas the refusal to tolerate non-democrats would be designed to protect democracy, the refusal to tolerate liars ("on pain of being excluded from the community of practical reasoners," or for some similar canting reason) would only be for the protection of ethics on a stipulative definition of ethics: even perhaps on a definition which betrays a closet transcendentalist realism.

J. Cease-fire and Apologia

However inadequate this essay may be, the real oddity about it seems to be less its philosophical weaknesses than the fact that it was composed at all. It is designed, after all, to expose and attempt to correct a rather mysterious phenomenon, that of a group of theistic, indeed Christian, philosophers who act as though it makes no great difference in ethics whether God exists at all, who seem inclined to assume that the question of whether there can be moral truths at all in his absence can be lightly put aside. Against that kind of mentality, which at best denotes a compartmentalized lifestyle in which teaching in a University has nothing to do with

worship or living the good life, at worst a subordi-
nation of truth to comfort and careerism, I have set
the Augustinian and generally patristic view that the
success of Christian thinking in solving dilemmas
insurmountable within the domain of purely secular philosophy is a strong argument for its truth;
and one would suppose, if for its truth, also for its
importance.

To the objection, implicit or explicit, that Christian philosophers should find no comfort in retiring to their own intellectual ghetto, I have made a
partial reply, which can now be taken a little further, and to which a second and complementary
point should be added. The partial reply was that, if
we are convinced of the role of God in ethics, we
should find it no surprise that the subject is at present
in the kind of chaos which has now been widely
recognized. That being so, further detailed and careful examination of non-theistic possibilities can only
be to the theist's advantage. They will show the dead-
end which has been reached, and that, though Parfit
was certainly right in trying to isolate a new and
wholly atheist ethic, purged of its Christian roots,
the development of that ethic, or rather the attempts
to develop it, can only be predicted as liable to ag-
gravate the chaos. In other words the net result of
such enquiries, we can be sure, will be to increase
the bleakness and despair in any observer of the scene
who is not emotionally committed to the view that
the Non-religious Ethic is the only possible show in
town. For he will recognize that the only roads out
of that bleakness are the theistic road or the road of
lying and deception (even self-deception) in the in-

terest of a minimum of social stability: a sort of philosophical vanguard theory, as roughly desiderated by
Sidgwick.

Curiously enough we are back once again to an
Augustinian *topos*. As we observed, in abandoning
his chair of rhetoric in Milan, Augustine said he was
giving up a chair of lying. By choosing Christian
theism over such lying—not least was it the job of
such professors to utter specious panegyrics of the
Emperor and the government in the interests of promoting self-indulgence, self-satisfaction (in the
Emperor), and social stability—Augustine has set a
bold example. And an example in another sense as
well. I observed earlier that one of the explanations
of why theists wish to play down their theism is that
they want to be able to debate, at best in a generous
spirit, with their secular opponents. But such gen-
erosity may, and I believe often is, a mask— in
Nietzsche's sense—for something much more allur-
ingly sinister. To get on in professional philosophy
there seem to be at least two requirements. One of
these is to be a seeker for truth; the other is to get
one's Ph.D., to secure an appointment in a philosophy department, to get tenure and all the rest of the
glittering and not so glittering prizes. Needless to
say, these two requirements may be in conflict, if
not often incompatible, and they provide a test of
practical, if not of theoretical ethics. The Christian
philosopher will, and will increasingly, find himself
tempted to run for cover in the secular world of
post-Christian ethics. At best he may come to re-
semble Plato's portrait of the philosopher taking
shelter beneath the wall as the storm rages by. It

requires, and will require, a little courage to attempt
to be a Catholic philosopher in an increasingly hostile world. In itself, that should not be a discouragement; after all courage is one of the traditional virtues. A second reason then for not succumbing to
the temptation to retreat into an intellectual ghetto
is that by doing so we loose the opportunity to
exercize that virtue.

But things are never as simple as they seem. To
leave the intellectual ghetto does not mean cutting
ourselves off from our own intellectual roots. There
is nothing more ludicrous than the Christian who,
despising the Eurocentrism which some wrongly
malign in his religion, engages in high-minded dialogue with exponents of other traditions without
any serious knowledge of his own. In the eyes of the
more honourable members of such other traditions
(including the tradition of secularism) such Christians are merely sad, to the more cynical they are
useful idiots.

Instead of courage in moral debate (as in moral
practice), there is always the possibility of going
along (If you want to go up, go along, as one of the
Watergate conspirators put it). And that going along
can be rationalized. If I do not get this appointment
because I am counter-cultural (and Christianity is
counter-cultural in our world, as in Augustine's,
though not in that of Aquinas), someone much
worse, from the Christian point of view, will be ap-
pointed. I remember a cartoon of Mrs Thatcher at a
political rally. "If we don't sell arms to the apartheid
régime," she screams, "some bloody corrupt for-
eigner will." More seriously, I should conclude by

noticing that all one is asking of the theist is that he not compromise with the truth about ethics as the price of apparent success, intellectual or other. Stubbornness in itself is no virtue; knowing what cannot be compromised in a hostile environment certainly is. Otherwise Socrates would not have drunk hemlock, Thomas More would not have lost his head, and Jesus would not have been crucified.

John M. Rist
Cambridge, England

Notes

[1] See M. D. Chenu, *La Théologie comme science au XIIIème siècle* (Paris: J. Vrin, 1969).

[2] The misleading phrase is particularly associated with Alan Donagan; *The Theory of Morality* (Chicago: University of Chicago Press, 1977). It is misleading because it reflects a historical rather than a philosophical truth.

[3] Cf. an informative passage of Galen cited by R. Walzer, *Galen on Jews and Christians* (Oxford: Oxford University Press, 1949), p. 48.

[4] C. Taylor, *Sources of the Self* (Cambridge, MA: Harvard University Press, 1989).

[5] I take it that this is the point of what J. L. Mackie calls an "error theory"; *Ethics: Inventing Right and Wrong* (Harmondsworth, NY: Penguin, 1977), chapter 1.

[6] The (characteristically utilitarian) view of H. Sidgwick, *The Methods of Ethics* (London: Macmillan, 1907⁸), p. 490.

[7] B. Williams and A. K. Sen, *Utilitarianism and Beyond* (Cambridge: Cambridge University Press, 1982), p. 16.

[8] From the philosophical point of view it might be interesting (to identify the limits of perfection) to have a Steroid Olympics in which all the athletes could take as many drugs as they could gorge; but presumably that is to be forbidden as *curiositas*.

[9] H. Frankfurt, *The Importance of What We Care About* (Cambridge: Cambridge University Press, 1988), pp. 185-188.

[10] Joachim C. Fest, *The Face of the Third Reich* (Harmondsworth, NY: Penguin, 1979), p. 316.

[11] See George Steiner, *Real Presences* (Chicago: University of Chicago Press, 1989) for the idea that an attack on meaning is necessarily an antitheistic move.

102 JOHN M. RIST

[12] P. Fussell, *Wartime: Understanding and Behaviour in the Second World War* (Oxford: Oxford University Press, 1989) p. 132.

[13] J. Rawls, *Political Liberalism* (New York: Columbia University Press, 1993), with the comments of J. Haldane, "The Individual, the State and the Common Good," *Social Philosophy and Policy* 13 (1996): 59-79.

[14] Cf. P. Geach, "The Moral Law and the Law of God" (originally from *God and the Soul*), in P. Helm (ed.), *Divine Commands and Morality* (Oxford: Oxford University Press, 1981), pp. 172-173. Geach's remarks are interesting, though I should not wish entirely to endorse them.

[15] E.g., J. M. Finnis, *Natural Law and Natural Rights* (Oxford: Oxford University Press, 1980), chapter 13.

[16] That it is not so *misused* is well argued by B. Ashley, "What is the End of the Human Person? The Vision of God and Integral Human Fulfilment," in L. Gormally (ed.), *Moral Truth and Moral Tradition* (Dublin: Four Courts Press, 1994), pp. 68-96.

[17] I shall return to the wider sense of "religious" shortly.

[18] D. Parfit, *Reasons and Persons* (Oxford: Clarendon Press, 1986), pp. 453-454.

[19] Aristotle's "fine" may have more resemblance to one of Moore's non-natural qualities. How would that make it less Platonic? Moore's qualities are non-causal, and they are qualities of substances, not substances, while Plato's Forms are both causal and possessed of what Aristotle realized are substantive characteristics. That is why Platonism needs completion by the assimilation of Forms to something which may be called "God," for qualities (as Plotinus and Augustine had learned) exist in a substance (A Form exists in a mind). As for Moore's non-natu-

ral qualities, Plato himself would say that if they are in the world they must have "come-to-be." They must depend on a cause (including a "formal" cause) outside our (natural) "world."

[20]L. W. Sumner, *The Moral Foundation of Rights* (Oxford: Clarendon Press, 1987), especially chapter 4 which discusses Bentham's attack on natural rights (as proposed by Locke) as "absurd in logic" and "pernicious in morals." On p.117 Sumner notes that Locke realized that a natural rights theory presupposes a natural theology. Notice the comments of S. Darwall, *Philosophical Ethics* (Boulder, CO: Westview Press, 1998), p. 10.

[21]It is perplexing that Parfit shows no interest in considering whether we might be (inter alia) soulbodies of a roughly Aristotelian type.

[22]I am hoping to discuss such matters further in a book on ethical foundationalism.

[23]*Reasons and Persons*, p. 443.

[24]*Ethics: Inventing Right and Wrong*, especially chapter 1.

[25]In a paper on Plato's metaethics in the Republic (to be published in the Proceedings of the Boston Area Colloquium in Ancient Philosophy) I suggested that all moral philosophers are of two kinds, those who advocate something like traditional objective morality and those who prefer morality substitutes. My commentator (Prof. Rachel Barney) dismissed this as "hopelessly Procrustean," but I am not impressed, and I hope shortly (as I say in my paper) to defend my view at book length, urging that in ethics the relationship between objective transcendentalism of a broadly platonic sort and alternative "moralities" resembles that between natural and positive law. The one depends on the nature of

God, the other on the decisions of men.

[26] See K. J. Clark (ed.), in *Philosophers who Believe* (Downers Grove, IL: Inter Varsity Press, 1993), p. 16.

[27] For the history see especially R.Sorabji, *Aristotle Transformed* (Ithaca: Cornell University Press, 1990).

[28] A. MacIntyre, *After Virtue* (Notre Dame: Notre Dame University Press, 1981), pp. 6-22.

[29] This is not the place to offer a lengthy account of the relation between divine commands and morality. Suffice it to say that a theist must be able to give not one but two partial answers to the question, Why should this action be done? The answers propose conditions for right action. They are (1) because it is good, and (2) because it is ordered by God. (Note that in the *Timaeus* Plato offered two analogous answers to the question, Why did a [good] demiurge form the world? The answers are (1) because he wanted to, and (2) because he is good.)

[30] I have considered some of the attractions of lying and deception for the political classes more specifically in "Democracy and Religious Values: Augustine on Locke, Lying and Individualism," *Augustinian Studies* 29 (1998): 7-24. For Augustine's own views about the use and misuse of rhetoric, see R. Dodaro, "Eloquent Lies, Just War and the Politics of Persuasion: Reading Augustine's *City of God* in a 'Postmodern' World," *Augustinian Studies* 25 (1994): 77-137.

The Aquinas Lectures
Published by the Marquette University Press
Milwaukee WI 53201-1881 USA
*Volumes marked * are avaiable as e-books. See web page.*

1. *St. Thomas and the Life of Learning.* John F. McCormick, S.J. (1937) 0-87462-101-1

2. *St. Thomas and the Gentiles.* Mortimer J. Adler (1938) 0-87462-102-X

3. *St. Thomas and the Greeks.* Anton C. Pegis (1939) 0-87462-103-8

4. *The Nature and Functions of Authority.* Yves Simon (1940) 0-87462-104-6

5. *St. Thomas and Analogy.* Gerald B. Phelan (1941) 0-87462-105-4

6. *St. Thomas and the Problem of Evil.* Jacques Maritain (1942) 0-87462-106-2

7. *Humanism and Theology.* Werner Jaeger (1943) 0-87462-107-0

8. *The Nature and Origins of Scientism.* John Wellmuth (1944) 0-87462-108-9

9. *Cicero in the Courtroom of St. Thomas Aquinas.* E.K. Rand (1945) 0-87462-109-7

10. *St. Thomas and Epistemology.* Louis-Marie Regis, O.P. (1946) 0-87462-110-0

11. *St. Thomas and the Greek Moralists.* Vernon J.Bourke (1947) 0-87462-111-9

12. *History of Philosophy and Philosophical Education.* Étienne Gilson (1947) 0-87462-112-7

13. *The Natural Desire for God.* William R.O'Connor (1948) 0-87462-113-5

14. *St. Thomas and the World State.* Robert M. Hutchins (1949) 0-87462-114-3

15. *Method in Metaphysics.* Robert J. Henle, S.J. (1950) 0-87462-115-1

16. *Wisdom and Love in St. Thomas Aquinas.* Étienne Gilson (1951) 0-87462-116-X

17. *The Good in Existential Metaphysics.* Elizabeth G. Salmon (1952) 0-87462-117-8

18. *St. Thomas and the Object of Geometry.* Vincent E. Smith (1953) 0-87462-118-6

19. *Realism And Nominalism Revisted.* Henry Veatch (1954) 0-87462-119-4

20. *Imprudence in St. Thomas Aquinas.* Charles J. O'Neil (1955) 0-87462-120-8

21. *The Truth That Frees.* Gerard Smith, S.J. (1956) 0-87462-121-6

22. *St. Thomas and the Future of Metaphysics.* Joseph Owens, C.Ss.R. (1957) 0-87462-122-4

23. *Thomas and the Physics of 1958: A Confrontation.* Henry Margenau (1958) 0-87462-123-2

24. *Metaphysics and Ideology.* Wm. Oliver Martin (1959) 0-87462-124-0

25. *Language, Truth and Poetry.* Victor M. Hamm (1960)
0-87462-125-9

26. *Metaphysics and Historicity.* Emil L. Fackenheim (1961)
0-87462-126-7

27. *The Lure of Wisdom.* James D. Collins (1962)
0-87462-127-5

28. *Religion and Art.* Paul Weiss (1963) 0-87462-128-3

29. *St. Thomas and Philosophy.* Anton C. Pegis (1964)
0-87462-129-1

30. *The University in Process.* John O. Riedl (1965)
0-87462-130-5

31. *The Pragmatic Meaning of God.* Robert O. Johann (1966)
0-87462-131-3

32. *Religion and Empiricism.* John E. Smith (1967)
0-87462-132-1

33. *The Subject.* Bernard Lonergan, S.J. (1968)
0-87462-133-X

34. *Beyond Trinity.* Bernard J. Cooke (1969) 0-87462-134-8

35. *Ideas and Concepts.* Julius R. Weinberg (1970)
0-87462-135-6

36. *Reason and Faith Revisited.* Francis H. Parker (1971)
0-87462-136-4

37. *Psyche and Cerebrum.* John N. Findlay (1972)
0-87462-137-2

38. *The Problem of the Criterion.* Roderick M. Chisholm (1973)
0-87462-138-0

39. *Man as Infinite Spirit.* James H. Robb (1974)
0-87462-139-9

40. *Aquinas to Whitehead: Seven Centuries of Metaphysics of Religion.* Charles Hartshorne (1976) 0-87462-141-0

41. *The Problem of Evil.* Errol E. Harris (1977)
0-87462-142-9

42. *The Catholic University and the Faith.* Francis C. Wade, S.J. (1978) 0-87462-143-7

43. *St. Thomas and Historicity.* Armand J. Maurer, C.S.B. (1979) 0-87462-144-5

44. *Does God Have a Nature?* Alvin Plantinga (1980)
0-87462-145-3

45. *Rhyme and Reason: St. Thomas and Modes of Discourse.* Ralph Mcinerny (1981) 0-87462-148-8

46. *The Gift: Creation.* Kenneth L. Schmitz (1982)
0-87462-149-6

47. *How Philosophy Begins.* Beatrice H. Zedler (1983)
0-87462-151-8

48. *The Reality of the Historical Past.* Paul Ricoeur (1984)
0-87462-152-6

49. *Human Ends and Human Actions: An Exploration in St. Thomas' Treatment.* Alan Donagan (1985) 0-87462-153-4

50. *Imagination and Metaphysics in St. Augustine.* Robert O'Connell, S.J. (1986) 0-87462-227-1

51. *Expectations of Immortality in Late Antiquity.* Hilary A Armstrong (1987) 0-87462-154-2

52. *The Self.* Anthony Kenny (1988) 0-87462-155-0

53. *The Nature of Philosophical Inquiry.*Quentin Lauer, S.J. (1989) 0-87562-156-9

54. *First Principles, Final Ends and Contemporary Philosophical Issues.* Alasdair MacIntyre (1990) 0-87462-157-7

55. *Descartes among the Scholastics.* Marjorie Greene (1991) 0-87462-158-5

56. *The Inference That Makes Science.*Ernan McMullin (1992) 0-87462-159-3

57. *Person and Being.* W. Norris Clarke, S.J. (1993) 0-87462-160-7

58. *Metaphysics and Culture.* Louis Dupré (1994) 0-87462-161-5

59.* *Mediæval Reactions to the Encounters between Faith and Reason.* John F. Wippel (1995) 0-87462-162-3

60.* *Paradoxes of Time in Saint Augustine.* Roland J. Teske, S.J. (1996) 0-87462-163-1

61.* *Simplicity As Evidence of Truth.* Richard Swinburne (1997) 0-87462-164-X

62. *Science, Religion and Authority: Lessons from the Galileo Affair.* Richard J. Blackwell. (1998) 0-87462-165-8

63.* *What Sort of Human Nature? Medieval Philosophy and the Systematics of Christology.* Marilyn McCord Adams. (1999) 0-87462-166-6

64.* *On Inoculating Moral Philosophy against God.* John M. Rist. (2000) 0-87462-XXX-X.

About the Aquinas Lecture Series

The Annual St. Thomas Aquinas Lecture Series began at
Marquette University in the Spring of 1937. Ideal for classroom use, library additions, or private collections, the
Aquinas Lecture Series has received international acceptance by scholars, universities, and libraries. Hardbound
in maroon cloth with gold stamped covers. Uniform style
and price ($15 each). Some reprints with soft covers.
Complete set (64 Titles) (ISBN 0-87462-150-X) receives
a 40% discount. New standing orders receive a 30% discount. Regular reprinting keeps all volumes available. Or-
dering information (purchase orders, checks, and major
credit cards accepted):

Bookmasters Distribution Services
30 Amberwood Parkway
P.O. Box 2139
Ashland OH 44805
     Order Toll-Free (800) 247-6553
     FAX: (419) 281 6883

Editorial Address:
Dr. Andrew Tallon, Director
Marquette University Press
Box 1881
Milwaukee WI 53201-1881
Tel: (414) 288-7298 FAX: (414) 288-3300
email: andrew.tallon@marquette.edu.

http://www.mu.edu/mupress/

Subscribe to the free *MU Press Enewsletter* for immediate notice of new books. With the word **subscribe** as the subject,
email a message to universitypress@marquette.edu

ISBN 0-87462-167-4

51500